Second Edition

Literacy and Education

Understanding the New Literacy Studies in the Classroom

Kate Pahl and Jennifer Rowsell

Los Angeles | London | New Delhi
Singapore | Washington DC

First published 2005, reprinted in 2006, 2007, 2008 twice, 2009, 2011 twice, 2013.

SAGE Publications Ltd
1 Oliver's Yard
55 City Road
London EC1Y 1SP

SAGE Publications Inc.
2455 Teller Road
Thousand Oaks, California 91320

SAGE Publications India Pvt Ltd
B 1/I 1 Mohan Cooperative Industrial Area
Mathura Road
New Delhi 110 044

SAGE Publications Asia-Pacific Pte Ltd
3 Church Street
#10-04 Samsung Hub
Singapore 049483

Library of Congress Control Number: 2011940055

British Library Cataloguing in Publication data

A catalogue record for this book is available from the British Library

ISBN 978-1-4462-0134-3
ISBN 978-1-4462-0135-0 (pbk)

Typeset by C&M Digitals (P) Ltd, Chennai, India
Printed and bound by MPG Printgroup, UK
Printed on paper from sustainable resources

Contents

List of figures

Foreword

In a time of rampant standardization of literacy education through government insistence of measurable performance outcomes in many countries, it is restorative to read Kate Pahl's and Jennifer Rowsell's new edition of *Literacy and Education*. Their book begins as it continues with a thought-provoking vignette written by a high school student, a survivor of the Haiti earthquake of 2010, who came to Princeton hopeful of studying at Rutgers University. His writing tells of privileges and silences, about places at the centre, places at the margins, about untold stories. Pahl and Rowsell populate their guide to the New Literacy Studies with students and teachers making meanings of and in their worlds. Importantly, they show that developing literate repertoires involves complex relationships with identity, time, spaces and places – material and virtual.

Allan Luke wrote in the Foreword to the first edition in 2005 that *Literacy and Education* 'is a comprehensive introduction to social and cultural approaches to literacy' (Luke, 2005) which leads us to young people and teachers negotiating the everyday worlds of classrooms and communities. This remains true of the new edition. Writing for teachers, Pahl and Rowsell cover significant theoretical and research terrain; they are flamboyant tour guides, ranging far and wide in their treatment of ideas as diverse as *artifactual critical literacy, communities of practice, design literacies, discourse, figured worlds, genre theory, materiality, modal learning, multimodality* and more. I mean flamboyant in the best sense of this word – that is, they lead us with flair, colour and surprise. The last 50 years of the best of theory and research in literacy education (and what is emerging) are signalled in their glossary and introduced in the book! Their vignettes adroitly illustrate these new vocabularies, giving us alternative words and generative metaphors as antidotes to the sometimes depressing world of literacy education policy. Pahl and Rowsell re-energize the reader; their stories make you want to go back to the classroom, the library, the neighbourhood walk, the mall, the Internet – to watch how young people are making meaning and how teachers are approaching their pedagogies in these new times.

So why would teachers, early career and those all along the way, and teacher educators want to read such a book given that typical literacy policy agenda at this time requires narrow approaches to literacy teaching and in some cases provides teachers with scripted curriculum? Pahl and Rowsell are generous tour guides, offering teachers a rich intellectual journey into the world of New Literacy Studies, the work of seminal theorists such as Hymes, Heath, Street and Kress, to their own work and that of leading and emergent scholars. They introduce historical and contemporary research from literacy educators far and wide – from South Africa, to Canada, to Australia, to New Zealand and the United Kingdom – working in very different contexts with highly diverse students. They actively mediate and translate complex and rich ideas, often through illustrative stories from their own and others' practice. Having worked with teacher-researchers for over three decades, I see this as a book to be read in such collectives, shared with other teachers, as the impetus for classroom investigations. It is a text that opens up action and inquiry. The teachers with whom I have worked for some time do not avoid theory or research; instead they welcome it, finding that it provides rich nourishment in what is sometimes a barren educational landscape. However, increasingly they are time-poor and somewhat exhausted by compulsory change initiatives and mandated literacy programmes. This book is a valuable offering to such practitioners. It offers tools to deconstruct different views of teaching and learning, and to undertake ongoing research about their practices. Further, it offers a persuasive rationale for including complex multimodal approaches to literacy in today's globally mediated environments, which young people must navigate.

For teacher educators, *Literacy and Education* is a really useful resource as it helps tell the history of literacy education studies even as it invites new readers and new teachers into possible futures. The fascinating fragments from vignettes, classrooms and communities provide a conduit for examining complex theoretical perspectives, different paradigms and contemporary debates in literacy education. The theory boxes, reflections, activities, vignettes and questions are pedagogical tools, soundly underpinned with theory and not simply layout options. Having a comprehensive research-based text around which innovative pedagogies and classroom projects can be designed can facilitate the considerable identity work that new teachers need to undertake.

Importantly, given the demands of the times in terms of measurable standards, Pahl and Rowsell argue that 'it is possible to combine an understanding of literacy as a set of skills with an understanding of how we use literacy in everyday life'. Informed by inclusive models of literacy, such as those conceptualized by Bill Green (including operational, cultural and critical dimensions) and Luke and Freebody's four resources approach, addressing skills remains just one element of teachers' work, but not the whole deal. Pahl and Rowsell recognize the ways in which texts increasingly frame and organize people's lives and invite teachers to use their own classroom materials, bookshelves and so on as a place to start in thinking about how texts capture 'traces of practice'.

A key idea that underlies much of the unique work accomplished by Pahl and Rowsell is that of artifactual literacies. The focus not only on different media and modes, as well various texts and genres, but also on the very objects or *stuff* that people use to make meaning – whether it is the craftwork done at home, the design work done by film-makers, the shoe-boxes redecorated and story-filled and brought to school – as ethnographers of literacy they never take the everyday for granted. Rather, in rendering it visible, they raise new questions for educators about curriculum design, what values are preferred. How to think critically about new domains of practice, in particular multimodal sites, is a really useful contribution for teachers who wish to incorporate digital communications and new media. Noting the dilemmas teachers face when out-of-school texts enter the classroom, they demonstrate how the child's resources may act as an important interface between existing knowledge and experience and new academic discursive practices.

One of the most generative frames of reference over the past two decades for considering the learning assets in children's worlds beyond the school was developed by Luis Moll and colleagues (1992). Funds of knowledge are the resources shared in families and local communities. For example, such knowledge may range from horticulture, cooking, mechanics, music, herbal medicine, and so on. Such knowledge may be in various ways connected to the locality of the community. People make use of what they have to hand in similar ways to how children necessarily use the resources they have to make meaning in classrooms. The extent to which there is permeability between home and school worlds can help children to feel as though they belong and accomplish new learning. Pahl and Rowsell review recent related international research on the various ways in which parents in different communities support their children's literacy. They consider how schools can open their practices to allow for multilingual literacy events such as dual-language story books. They also consider how teachers can be more open to learning from home practices, for example to learn about how families engage with a range of technologies.

Increasingly, scholars are recognizing the need to go beyond their disciplines and to employ multiple research approaches to answer research questions. In this book we see the value of the careful ethnographic work which underpins the New Literacy Studies, the inclusion of teacher inquiry for social justice, for which there is a long tradition in literacy studies (Rogers et al., 2009), plus the inclusion of new approaches, such as Alison Clark's (2010) work with children and space, which open up new frames of reference. The authors understand that what is needed is an ecological approach to the study of literacy, focusing on how people make meaning in relation to their own identities and localities with the resources at hand. This leads Pahl and Rowsell to suggest very creative projects for teachers to undertake at home and at school with respect to the ecologies of print-related objects in homes and schools which take into account the power relations that pertain to language and spatial practices. Teacher readers would benefit from reading this book in small study groups as it is designed to generate activity and inquiry, ideally where schools are 'hubs for research on literacy'.

New Literacy Studies researchers have always concerned themselves with context. Indeed, a key assumption of their approach is the importance of situating literacy studies in connection with wider cultural practices and avoiding the assumption that literacy is what is taught and learned in school (Street & Street, 1991). Recently given features of the contemporary era, in association with globalization (mobility, environmental disasters, financial crises), literacy scholars have attended not only to context as a setting for the negotiation of practices, but to space and place as constitutive categories in their own right. Just as we understand that discourse is constitutive of identities, for example a 'refugee' in comparison to 'illegal' or 'alien', now literacy educators are looking again at spatial relationships and also at how places are made by people and how such relationships might afford new place-based critical literacies (Comber, 2010). Even in these words alone, we can see how identity, power, space and place come together in our naming practices and legal discourses.

People's identities cannot be separated from the ways they engage in literate practices; their histories and present positioning in places and spatial relations infuse how they make sense of and compose texts. Their biographical resources are therefore crucial to what might be done in schools and other sites of learning. Yet over time people's interests and capabilities change as they connect with and take on new opportunities, thereby layering both identities and discursive resources. Schooled identities can allow for opening out and enriching of possibilities or they can lock people into different educational trajectories. Pahl and Rowsell invite us to look closely at the interpretative resources children have, to see multilingualism as an asset, not a problem in learning to read. Their classrooms of tomorrow are rich with potential for teachers and children to research in various settings, to interrogate, to debate, to work collaboratively, to engage in intercultural communication. In short, they would be developing complex dispositions towards inquiry, analysis, design and action. Literacy is not a discreet academic skill but part of a complex and dynamic learner repertoire (Comber, 2007; Janks, 2010).

In an era of ever-changing digital communications, audit cultures and high-stakes literacy assessment, it is more important than ever to create spaces where teachers can engage intellectually with the new demands of teaching literacy and the contradictions that lie in normative educational discourses. Abstract notions of performance tend to bracket out embodied people in particular places. So-called improvement in literacy becomes just a matter of investing in the right programme or applying the correct techniques to solve the diagnosed problem. Meanwhile the real game, in the world beyond schooling, has moved on in terms of accessing design literacies and modal learning. There are real equity issues here, as Pahl and Rowsell note. Wisely, they do not advocate for a lack of attention to traditional literate practices, such as composing well. However, they argue cogently for an equal prioritization of the complex semiotic repertoires upon which the full participation of citizens depends. They are aware that there is a danger in the contemporary moment of one kind of literacy – the old basics – being offered to poor, working-class and immigrant children under the auspices of education, while more affluent children assemble new digital media literacies at home and at school, exponentially gaining an advantage over peers with less access to the newly dominant communication practices.

Literacy and Education makes an important contribution to the field of literacy studies. I have described it here as a guide book because it tells us where we have been, outlines the features of where we are now and points the way for where we need to go as an educational community – teachers and researchers working together – committed to literacy education for social justice. Importantly, as guides to the New Literacy Studies, they offer hope for more equitable literacy learning, hope that in part emanates from the fresh perspective of their rich research repertoires which allow for new pedagogical designs, new literacies and new ecologies.

Barbara Comber
Queensland University of Technology, Brisbane

About the authors

Kate Pahl is a Reader in Literacies in Education at the Department of Educational Studies, University of Sheffield. She has published widely in the fields of family literacy, the New Literacy Studies, and home and intergenerational literacy practices within families. She is involved in policy and practice in the field of family literacy and home book sharing practices. Her recent research includes an ethnographic study of family book sharing practices, funded by Booktrust, UK and a study called 'Writing in the Home and in the Street' funded by the AHRC, UK.

Jennifer Rowsell is a Canada Research Chair in Multiliteracies at Brock University in Canada. During her time at Rutgers Graduate School of Education, she conducted three longitudinal studies and served as Coordinator of the English Education program. Jennifer has co-written and written books in such areas as family literacy, early literacy, New Literacy Studies, and multimodality. Her research is concerned with exploring multimodal and artifactual epistemologies in a variety of learning contexts.

Acknowledgements

We have benefited from the input and ideas of the following people: Chloe Allan, Donna Alvermann, Fiona Blaikie, Margit Boeck, Robin Bone, Deborah Bullivant, Cathy Burnett, Catherine Compton-Lilly, Julia Davies, Bill Green, Abigail Hackett, Mary Hamilton, Danuta Harrap, Marcus Hurcombe, Diane Lapp, Joanne Larson, Mary Lovering, Jackie Marsh, Guy Merchant, Bonny Norton, the Qaddar family, Steve Pool, Zahir Rafiq, Sherry Rose, Richard Steadman-Jones, Brian Street, Maureen Walsh, Pam Whitty and Angela Wright.

We would like to thank our funders: The Arts and Humanities Research Council (AHRC), UK (Connected Communities), Booktrust, UK, The Museums and Libraries Association (MLA) Yorkshire, UK, the International Reading Association's Elva Knight Grant, the Social Science and Humanities and Research Council (SSHRC), Canada, and Yorkshire Forward, UK.

We are deeply grateful to the following scholars for their vignettes: Sandra Abrams, Parven Akhter, Eryn Decoste, Candace Kuby, Cheryl McLean, Lynn Marr, Sue Nichols, Rahat Niqvi, Anne Peel, Francene Planas, Rob Simon, Saskia Stille, Kari-Lynn Winters and Amelia Wolfe.

We would like to thank the following young people for their work and ideas: Bonni, Dionne, Lucy and Tanya, Winston Charlebon and the Year 6 children from High Greave School, Rotherham as well as the Year 6 children from Thorogate Junior School, Rotherham.

Finally, we would like to thank Marianne Lagrange and Nicola Marshall for their support during the editorial process as well as Barbara Comber for her thoughtful response to our work in the Foreword.

Glossary of terms

Affordance
Choosing materials appropriately for the task, for example, choosing a font for a poster which carries effect.

Anthropology
The study of people in everyday, naturalistic contexts, focused on cultures and practices.

Artifact
An object that is tied to a context and an identity. It carries a story and has a past. For example, framed photographs.

Artifactual critical literacy
Looking at objects from the perspective of power, discourse and ideology.

Autonomous
A model of literacy independent of social context. Literacy as a set of skills. For example, phonics programmes, reading schemes.

Avatars
Characters who have digital identities such as Harry Potter in the Harry Potter videogames.

Communicational landscape
The different ways people make meaning, in either visual or verbal forms. For example, the Internet offers a vast array of communicational sites.

Communities of practice
Groups of people with common beliefs, values, ways of speaking and being. We all belong to a number of them. For example, home, school, office, etc.

Constraint
The things that stop texts being functional. For example, texts that are too linguistic for pre-school children.

Critical literacy
A way of looking at the embodied understandings within texts as opposed to a surface reading of texts. Seeing power within texts. For

example, differentiating between two newspapers, such as *The Observer* and *The Daily Mail.*

Crossing

Moving from one site to the next. For example, home to school.

Cultural capital

The currency we bring to situations. For example, children bring experiences from home to school.

Cultural practices

The things we do with culture, the actions that take place around culture and the re-fashioning of culture in texts and artifacts. For example, parents making books with children on the web.

Cultural resources

A way of recognizing what children bring to educational settings from their own cultural heritage. For example, bringing in new information to school about cultural events.

Culture

A way of describing a characteristic of human life by which people share values, behaviours, ways of speaking, ways of being. For example, football in the UK.

Design literacies

Spin, design, multimodality and participatory structures are the four core elements of the framework, and creativity, trial and error, remix and convergence are dispositions adopted when taking a design literacies approach to literacy teaching and learning.

Dialogic

A give-and-take situation, a type of discourse, a way of speaking. For example, an interview in a magazine.

Digital literacies

Literacy practices online, such as writing messages in Club Penguin or creating new avatars.

Digitized artifacts

Anything that can be viewed online. For example, blogs, wikis, Prezis that have a form and function.

discourse

Language in a social context. For example, the language of PGCE students.

Discourse
Language and other stuff. For example, gestures, clothes (e.g. that worn by bikers).

Discursive identity
The way we speak is tied to who we are, our identity in the world. For example, when we become a teacher we take on a specific discursive identity around teaching as opposed to, for example, mothering.

Domains
Domains are spaces or worlds where we use literacy. For example, work, home, school.

e-portfolios
A repository that students fill that is online and can be co-ordinated by a teacher or facilitator so that students can gain credits for their work.

Ecological
Ecological work captures the interdependence that happens within communities when people rely on resources in their immediate environment for everyday practices, including literacy practices.

Ethnography
The study of cultural identities and worlds which focuses on ways of recording those cultural identities, and standing away and drawing close to the experience.

Family literacy
Any activity that involves parents and children in literacy. Activities are often taught in school settings, with joint programmes for parents and children to enjoy.

Figured worlds
Collectively realized 'as-if' worlds that we inhabit. Figured worlds are opened up by artifacts. For example, a staffroom in a school is a figured world.

Funds of knowledge
The cultural resources that families and homes bring to other settings. For example, home stories brought to classrooms.

Global domains
Networks and entities that exist outside the local. For example, the Internet is a global network.

Global literacies
Literacy practices that are associated with globalization. For example, the language used within global banking institutions such as Lloyds Bank.

Globalization
The process of imposed networks and entities into local domains. For example, McDonalds in local domains.

Hybridity
Different cultural forms interacting in the same space. For example, two children in a playground incorporating North American English with Chinese.

Identity
A way of describing a sense of self that is in practice. For example, two literacy teachers chatting at a language and literacy conference.

Identity-in-practice
Identities as expressed in artifacts, texts and discourse. For example, your diary is an expression of your identity-in-practice.

Ideology
Any system of cultural meaning which is infused with power that seeps into practices and texts. For example, a newspaper with a liberal slant on issues.

Intercultural communication
Communication between cultures that informs practice. For example, using children's funds of knowledge in the classroom.

Listening methodologies
Ways of eliciting students' thoughts and ideas that involve active methodologies that are congruent with their existing practices. For example, walking tours and the use of visual methods.

Literacies
Ways of expressing meaning in linguistic forms across domains. For example, text messaging.

Literacy
Ways of making meaning with linguistic stuff in a communicative landscape. For example, early writing with a drawing.

Literacy event
Any action involving the comprehension of print. For example, writing a lesson plan.

Literacy of fusion
It is combining elements of linguistic and visual in order to create a text. For example, using PowerPoint for a presentation.

Literacy practices
Patterns of activity around literacy. For example, a guided reading session with a particular set of practices.

Local domains
It is the sense of place and neighbourhood that people inhabit. For example, community centres.

Macro
Activity at a strategic level, such as government action. For example, 'No Child Left Behind'.

Materiality
The stuff we use to make texts. For example, tissue paper to make a collage.

Meso
Activity at an intermediate level, such as a school policy document. For example, home–school reading policy.

Micro
Activity at a local level, such as teachers in classrooms. For example, a Year 5 teacher working with a student.

Modal learning
Making meaning through multiple modes or units of representation and communication.

Mode
A unit of meaning and representation.

Motivated sign
Infusing our identity into texts. For example, a child putting a particular colour of paint in a drawing.

Multilingual literacies
Different linguistic identities can be employed in the same space. For example, Arabic language practices functioning alongside English language practices.

Multilingualism
The employment of different linguistic identities in a particular space. For example, Punjabi, Urdu and English used in a home space.

Multiliteracies
Using different linguistic systems within the same space. For example, home–school book-making using different languages and dual texts.

Multimodal identity
Individuals using different stuff to make meaning. For example, choosing a particular font and layout for an academic paper.

Multimodal literacy
Literacy teaching and learning that takes account of *all* modes within texts of all kinds.

Multimodality
A way of making meaning that allows for different modes. For example, model-making as a form of communication.

Multiple literacies
Different linguistic systems working within the same space. For example, Chinese, Turkish and English students working on a language activity at a writing centre.

Narrative
The showing or the telling of these events and the mode selected for that to take place. For example, a story told in a cartoon strip.

New Literacy Studies
An approach to literacy and language learning that looks at how literacy is used in everyday life – from literacy events like guided reading at school to reading a newspaper in a café.

Out-of-school literacy practices
Practices which are not infused with literacy pedagogy. For example, children playing videogames.

Pedagogy
The inscribing into practice of teacherly activities. For example, building assessment strands into a unit.

Reader response
Being able to identify texts as crafted objects and being alert to the values and interests that texts have within them.

Recontextualization
Carrying practices across sites and putting them in a different context. For example, taking popular songs from the radio and inserting them into school discourse.

Ruling passions
The way people's interest affects their literacy practices. For example, gardening.

Schooled literacy
A notion of literacy practices tied to school learning. For example, homework.

Sedimented identities in texts
The concept of the layering or sedimenting of identities in texts over time. For example, a grandparent's story becoming a picture and then a written story.

Sign
A combination of meaning and form. For example, a road sign.

Site
A place that is specific. For example, a mosque.

Social practice
Cultural patterns and forms inscribed into everyday lives. For example, eating breakfast.

Space
An area in which something takes place. A space can be real or imagined. For example, a classroom or a chatroom.

Strategies
The way the powerful shape space and practices. For example, standardized assessment tests.

Symbol
A sign that refers to an idea. For example, Bonni's special note in Chapter two.

Synaesthesia
The blurring of different modes into one another. For example, seeing words as colours.

Syncretic literacy
Two different cultural practices merging in one literacy practice. For example, a reading scheme in a different cultural space.

Tactics
The ways people who live within institutionalized spaces manipulate them. For example, students who write on desks.

Teacher mediation
Inscribing of teacher identity into texts and practices. For example, teachers working with reading schemes.

Text
It is an articulation of a discourse. For example, a website for a clothing company.

Texts as artifacts
Texts that have a history or story of their making. For example, a photo album.

Third space
It is a space where students draw on different discourses that are in-between other domains. For example, drawing on knowledge acquired through doing bike stunts in the science classroom.

Traces
An inscription to access a history. For example, a novel carries traces of an author's experience and ideas.

Visual communication
Ways of expressing meaning in the visual. For example, television.

Wealth model
A wealth model of literacy acknowledges the cultural resources families bring to literacy, such as stories told across generations.

Weblogs
Identity-infused web spaces with personal messages and artifacts.

1

The New Literacy Studies and teaching literacy: Where we were and where we are going

The following vignette was written by a participant in a high school study. Using the principles of **New Literacy Studies** and **multimodality**, Winston found his way into writing.

Vignette: Rutgers admission letter

By Winston Charlebon (pseudonym)

For many years, the small Caribbean Island of Haiti has been shunned by the world. Children have been starving, families have been homeless and the government has been negligent. The murders will never be reprimanded; the kidnappers celebrate showing no remorse for their actions while they spend their ransoms on life's vices. The children's clothes are saturated with dirt; their hands are worn down from strenuous labor. Their shoes are torn and old, their feet are swollen and blistered from the countless miles they walk. Their evangelical families pray to God anxiously waiting his return. For them Judgment Day is a liberation from this terrible life they live. January 12, 2010 their prayers were not answered. Instead, an earthquake ravaged through the capital city. People ran trying to escape the flying debris. The elderly were too weak to run and could not evade a horrible fate. And children studying in their classrooms were crushed by heavy bricks and wood and could not even say goodbye to their loved ones. My loved ones were right in the midst of it. They were left with

(Cont'd)

literally nothing, not even their lives. People heard about the earthquake and read about the earthquake and read the news report but very few people actually know what is occurring in Haiti and in other countries today. That is why I co-founded the Multicultural Awareness Group in order to help educate my fellow peers about different cultures that they might know about. Rutgers University is a unique university because of its immense diversity. If I am fortunate enough to be accepted into this university, I intend to take advantage of its diversity and use it as an opportunity to educate others about cultures that most individuals have not heard of. For many years, the small quintessential town of Princeton has attracted people from all over the globe. The children have been well fed, their families live in big houses, and the government has always been extremely gracious towards them. Violence is almost unheard of and any crime is punished severely. The children wear the latest designer clothes. The most expensive and fine jewelry hug their necks and wrists. Their hands are soft and smooth. Their fingers are pampered and manicured. However this is not how I have lived in Princeton. I lived in a small house with 7 people to share three bedrooms. I would make my own dinner and didn't have anyone to do my work for me. If I am accepted into Rutgers University, I will be able to open the eyes of several other students to a variety of different cultures, which would greatly benefit the diverse environment.

Reprinted with permission from Winston, October 11, 2010

○━ Key themes in the chapter:

- Literacy as a social practice
- Literacy as an event and a set of practices
- Literacy as a global and local practice
- Literacy as faith-based
- Literacy as critical

INTRODUCTION

Imagine that you are teaching students, like Winston, who have been identified as 'underachieving in literacy'. These are young people who come from a number of different backgrounds. Jennifer first met Winston when he was in a 9th Grade support English class when he expressed little interest in reading and writing. When she encountered

Winston he was struggling in English class and he showed little interest in reading literature and 'the canon', Shakespeare and Homer, and writing formal essays were not his favoured literacy practices. In his out-of-school life, Winston listens to rap, hip-hop, contributes (constantly) to *Facebook*, and takes photographs of his neighbourhood.

- How would you teach Winston?

Four years after meeting Winston, he came to see Jennifer with his Dad to discuss what he needs to do to get accepted into Rutgers University. Winston was a different young man, more serious, confident, and mature. During our conversation, we talked about writing a short **narrative** that captured him and that gave a specific picture to the reader about how he would contribute to Rutgers. We talked about his family and his aspirations and what inspired these aspirations. What resulted from the conversation is the first vignette in this book as a powerful signifier of enacting how to understand New Literacy Studies in a classroom. Clearly, something shifted with Winston and his relationship with English and writing formal essays. Winston attributes his change of heart to a supportive family and to good teachers at his high school. Jennifer still corresponds with Winston, who did not end up at Rutgers University but at a university further afield and he is very happy. Winston's thoughtful narrative is very much in the spirit of New Literacy Studies, in that it demonstrates his awareness of:

- Lived cultural practice

- Local–global connections

- Identity issues

- Felt emotions

The vignette depicts the dramatic change Winston experienced as he completed high school. Jennifer recollects his gradual socialization and eventual enjoyment of English over his years in high school. The vignette begins a journey into key themes introduced in this chapter and themes that run throughout the book.

These themes are:

1 Literacy as ecologies. By ecology we mean that literacy exists in places, as a set of actions by particular individuals that is in a network of other actions around literacy.

2 Literacy is an embodied practice that requires movement and action (e.g., scrolling, tapping, reading, sliding) and as an embodied experience it requires more modes of representation than ever, i.e. multimodality.

3 Critical literacy has always been important, but it is more important than ever that we critically frame the diverse texts our students use.

4 Literacy is still hand-made and artifactual, and it relates to real worlds and embodied experience.

5 Writing takes place in the home, in the street and in the school. This activity can be invisible and is materialized in different ways such as gardening and textiles.

6 More than ever, literacy is about digital and immersive worlds. It is also about challenging the binaries between the online and offline.

7 Literacy exists within curricular objectives and frameworks. We can't forget as educators that we need to negotiate our own philosophies and understandings of practice with curricula objectives and in the book we try to mediate new ideas with more traditional notions, such as academic literacy.

8 **Literacy** has a different logic that we uncover in the book, a logic more in line with twenty-first-century needs and practices.

The view of literacy as a **social practice** has been around for some time now. In writing this second edition of *Literacy and Education*, it is clear that the field has indeed moved on. Our aim in the second edition is to update our accounts of New Literacy Studies to see how this understanding of literacy can be applied to classrooms in new times, with potentially more immediate demands than in 2005. In this chapter, the concepts behind the idea of literacy as a social practice will be explained and then contextualized within important studies that have contributed to the field, five years on. What continue to be central to New Literacy Studies are the key ideas of **literacy events** and **literacy practices**.

The moment of composing a **text** can be described as a literacy event, an event in which literacy forms a part. Now, five years on, it is even more pressing to open up a definition of text to any kind of entity from which an individual makes meaning. For instance, a contemporary literacy event might be writing on someone's *Facebook* wall about an event that happened and getting immediate feedback from friends and family. Part of the composing process for a text draws on a meaning maker's experience of literacy practices. Winston pulls on his experience of creating voice in narratives through deft attention to detail and using the correct register for the reader. Working within a persuasive narrative, Winston knows how to rhetorically structure his argument so that the reader recognizes his unique contribution to a place. This view of literacy as informed by patterns of practice can be contrasted with a view of literacy as a set of skills. In this book, we argue that it is possible to combine an understanding of literacy as a set of skills *with* an understanding of how we use literacy in everyday life. In fact, we argue that if we bring these understandings together, it helps. What is more, we consider how the idea of literacy as a social practice encourages our students' writing and reading development in classroom settings.

Winston's vignette is a fitting segue to look at contemporary New Literacy Studies because it illustrates that when students draw on cultural experiences they have had in their lives, *they have more fluency in their writing*. Students may come from different parts of the globe, and then learn within an urban space. They may live in a remote rural community, on an island, but be connected to the world through the Internet. If literacy is understood as a *global and social practice*, this helps us understand why children need to communicate not only across different cultures, but also in relation to changing global communication.

* How can Winston access fluent writing?

Here we explore ways of engaging students who have rich experience of the world in writing so that they can access academic literacy. When Winston drew on his own experience, **culture**, lived history to write his admission essay, he drew on his **identity** as a teenager and child who knows about the reality of a culture under tremendous strain and arduous conditions. He speaks Haitian dialect, and this history and culture informs his perspective. At the same time, Winston lived in Princeton, a privileged university town in the United States. Locating his global identity within his local identity brings power, force, the everyday into his narrative.

Students within everyday and global spaces need to both pull on their global identities and make a success for themselves within local learning contexts. Literacy very quickly moves between local and global. At one moment you can be having a *Facebook* conversation with your friend down the corridor and, in the next moment, you can be emailing your Granny in Buenos Aires. In the book, we signal the thread between the local and the global. In Chapter 4 the spatial nature of literacy is explored, and we consider how an understanding of place and space can help shape literacy practices. Power comes into these discussions, as place-based literacies are connected to more powerful or less powerful spaces (Comber, 2010).

When our students write and read, they infuse these practices into their identities. Literacy learners bring their identities into the making of meaning, and as they learn to read, or put marks on a page, their marks are inscribed with that experience. This book connects to new ideas about the relationship between literacy and identity and how this works in classrooms. You will also consider what this perspective does to aid classroom practice. Identities are complex, made up of hybrid and multiple experiences. Identities shape our literacy practices. These identity-infused literacy practices are then taken up in school and encounter different literacy practices.

- How can we ensure that our students' literacy practices in classrooms account for their identities out of school?

Thinking about Winston and the story that he recounts about the harsh reality of life in Haiti, especially after the earthquake, how does Winston's story inform and empower his narrative? His narrative is that much richer when we consider his experience, living among privilege and aware of disparities between his Haitian roots and his Princeton life. With details such as 'the murders will never be reprimanded; the kidnappers celebrate showing no remorse for their actions while they spend their ransoms on life's vices', Winston imbues power through detail and through negotiating his immediate life with his cultural roots. His use of such writing devices as parallelism, nuanced descriptions give the narrative meaning and heart.

〰 Points of Reflection

These techniques might prompt you to reflect on the following *key questions*:

- How are student literacy practices and lived experiences different from their in-school literacy practices?

- Are there links between home literacy practices and school literacy practices? If there are, what are these links?

- Do the teaching resources and strategies that you use speak to or not speak to your students' sense of identity?

These questions are the focus of this chapter. The next section explains the theory behind New Literacy Studies and how you can use these theories to understand literacy practices.

NEW LITERACY STUDIES: AN OVERVIEW

This section introduces you to some of the key thinkers in this field, which has been identified as the New Literacy Studies. There are a number of scholars who have looked at literacy in everyday life (Street, 1995; Gee, 1996; Barton & Hamilton, 1998; Gutiérrez & Rogoff, 2003; Lankshear & Knobel, 2006; Stein, 2007; Janks, 2010; Pahl & Rowsell, 2010). These scholars have drawn on research from communication and anthropology to look at the role of literacy in people's lives.

Research from the New Literacy Studies examines literacy practices, and literacy events, and many researchers have used its perspective to look at what people do with literacy. Because of studies looking at how people used literacy in everyday life, the concept of literacy began to be rethought. Previously, literacy was something associated with books and writing and with language schema in our minds, collected over time. Literacy was perceived as a set of skills, which were taught in schools. In the mid-1980s, literacy was recognized as a social practice, something that people do in everyday life, in their homes, at work and at school. For example, in an ethnographic study in Lancaster, researchers watched people write notes at allotment meetings and observed people read to their children, and write diaries, letters and poems at home for pleasure (Barton & Hamilton, 1998).

- What do you like to write for pleasure?

As an example, consider the *Facebook* description given earlier. If this is described in terms of literacy practices, it could look like this:

Literacy event	Literacy practice	Social practice
Sending a message	*Facebook* messaging	*Facebook*ing to a friend in the next corridor

A literacy event is the observed event, often most easily spotted in the classroom. When your students write and read, they are engaged in a set of literacy events. These events are often regular, and relate to the practices of reading and writing. A student will read a book as part of the literacy practice of book reading in the classroom.

- Think of a literacy event that you regularly observe in your classroom.

In considering the New Literacy Studies, the field has been shaped by an anthropological, ethnographic approach to data collection and analysis. **Anthropology** is the study of people in everyday contexts. Within literacy education, researchers have gone to particular contexts to think about literacy and to watch people, and then they write up their observations.

A critical point in the history of literacy was the debate between James Paul Gee and Catherine Snow about the National Reading Panel's report on early literacy. As a response to Snow et al's report, 'Preventing Reading Difficulties in Young Children' (1998), Gee (1999a) drew attention to the dearth of studies that take a socially situated account of early literacy. This debate was highlighted by Jim Cummins in our first edition of *Literacy and Education*. Cummins claimed: 'underlying the problems with the report, he [Gee] argued, was a conception of reading as a process that happened exclusively within the heads of individuals rather than as a social practice intimately dependent on context' (Pahl & Rowsell, 2005: 145). This debate is still an underlining concern in areas such as book sharing and picture books where the field starts from a contested paradigm. Looking across cultures, religions, races, book sharing is one way to become literate, but it is not the only way. What we have found in writing this second edition is that certain fields still privilege paradigms and models that narrow their scope.

For the rest of the chapter, we follow a progression of stages and researchers who moved the field of New Literacy Studies forward into several intersecting fields such as new literacies, **multiliteracies**, multimodality, and **digital literacies**.

DOMAINS AND PRACTICES

Mapping literacy practices across sites is a helpful way of viewing the variability of literacy practices across sites, and beyond strictly viewing literacy practices as school-based. **Spaces** offer people multiple identities. These different identities inform literacy practices. A study of literacy and space offers the opportunity to think about what people do with literacy in different spaces.

Theory Box: Sylvia Scribner and Michael Cole on literacy practices in different **domains**

Sylvia Scribner and Michael Cole were psychologists who studied the Vai people of West Africa, in Liberia. They wanted to understand the relationship between local cultural contexts and the learning of literacy. Unusually, the people they studied, the Vai, had invented an original writing system, which was learned outside school. The school language was English, and the schools for the Quran used Arabic. Scribner and Cole studied the different language practices within the different settings. They found that specific types of literacy practices affected how people learned things. Scribner and Cole taught us that there is not just one literacy, but many forms of literacy, all linked to different domains of practice. The published study, *The Psychology of Literacy*, became a key text in the history of the New Literacy Studies, in that for the first time literacy practices were described in different domains of practice (Scribner & Cole, 1981).

The word 'domain' refers to a particular space, or world, where literacy is practised (e.g., the Church, the school, the home). Researchers have identified a number of literacy practices within different domains. Multiple identities come to the fore in specific domains. You may express yourself differently in a formal letter written at work, than you do in an email written to a friend at home.

- Where do you locate literacy in your life?

 ## Activity

Domains of Literacy

Divide your world into domains (i.e., places where literacy is carried out, for example, home, workplace, community, and so on). Within each domain, write a brief account of the literacy events you engage in. Note which are different and which are the same. Make a list of social practices that underpin the identified event. Writing an email to a work colleague, for example, is linked to the social practice of emailing.

A **domain** can be identified with a way of being, and in many cases, as a set of cultural beliefs, or a worldview. Sometimes it is site-specific, such as in a school, with buildings, but sometimes literacy practices from one domain, such as school, cross to another, such as home. Homework is an example of a literacy practice that is from the school domain, but is carried out in the home **site**.

- Which literacy practices cross sites?

Theory Box: Brian V. Street on ideological and autonomous literacies

Working as a social anthropologist in Iran, Brian Street described literacy practices in different domains. He conducted fieldwork in the village where he lived, which focused on literacy practices in different domains. These included what he termed:

- *maktab* literacy, or literacy associated with Islam and taught in the local Quranic schools;

- *commercial* literacy, or the reading and writing used for the management of fruit sales in the local village;

- *school* literacy, associated with the state schools more recently built in the villages and located in the urban areas as well.

This description of literacy enabled Street to identify how particular views of literacy were linked to particular ways of thinking (Street, 1995). From this, Street developed the concepts of *ideological* and *autonomous* literacy. He argued that literacy has been viewed, in particular by government agencies, as a separate thing-like object, which people should acquire, as a set of decontextualized skills. This view of literacy sees literacy as a technical skill. Writing, in particular, can be viewed as an autonomous skill, which can be related to individual cognitive processes. Street identified this view with a certain governmental trend to think of literacy as a set of skills that can be acquired. However, this view of literacy did not take into consideration how people used literacy. Instead, he argued, the term ideological could be used to describe the way in which literacy is grounded in how it is used, and how it relates to power structures within society (Street, 1993b).

Street therefore challenged us not to see literacy as a neutral skill, but as a *socially situated practice*. This was a key insight within the field known as the New Literacy Studies.

Points of Reflection

When and where can literacy be regarded as shaped by cultural and ideological forces?

When is literacy regarded as a set of skills?

Consider ways in which literacy is described where you work, and how it is regarded.

How does it change when you consider it as a reflection of social and cultural practice?

Theory Box: Shirley Brice Heath on literacy events and literacy practices

In the 1970s, in the rural Carolinas, another area of literacy was being researched. Shirley Brice Heath and her team of researchers were considering how different communities used and interacted around literacy. *Ways with Words* described the different language and literacy practices of two communities in the rural Carolinas, USA. In the book, Heath contrasted a black community, Trackton, with a white working-class community, Roadville. Heath paid close attention to the way parents in these two communities spoke to their children, raised them, how they decorated their homes and how the children interacted with their parents. Then she looked at what happened when they went to school. In the case of both Trackton and Roadville children, there was a disjuncture between their home literacy practices and their school literacy practices. This was in contrast to the children from the town. Heath called the town community, Maintown. The children in Maintown were teachers' children, who had been raised and talked to in a way which echoed the norms of 'school' literacy. In order to understand how different ways of interacting contributed to different outcomes in literacy, Heath focused her study around the concept of *literacy events*, which she defined as 'any action sequence, involving one or more persons, in which the production and/or comprehension of print plays a role' (Heath, 1983: 386). This concept enabled Heath to understand in a contrastive way the different events and practices around literacy, by isolating specific instances. Heath also looked at communicative utterances and contrasted them across communities.

(Cont'd)

For example, Heath describes how an African-American 2½-year-old named Lem made an oral response to his experience of hearing a distant bell ring, which meshed with his experience of Church-going:

Way Far

Now

It a Church bell

Ringin'

Dey singin'

Ringin'

You hear it?

I hear it

Far

Now

(Heath, 1983: 170)

Heath isolated this piece of oral talk, almost a poem, as one that was deeply embedded within the community's oral traditions, but did not have a corresponding link to classrooms.

Heath's work led many researchers to look more closely at literacy practices in home and communities. In this chapter, we ask you to consider what Heath's study can tell you in your teaching.

- Can it be used to consider how the literacy practices of school contrast with those of your students' **out-of-school literacy practices**?

THE ETHNOGRAPHY OF COMMUNICATION

Heath's work emerged from a tradition called the *ethnography of communication*, which understood how it was possible to understand different communicative events in different settings. By combining **ethnography** – as a way of studying different contexts and grounded in a particular methodological frame – with communication – the study of how people communicate – the ethnography of communication conceived a richer understanding of literacy and language skills. This has relevance to institutional settings such as schools. Dell Hymes, in particular, was able to describe why African-American children sometimes were not succeeding in schools. African-American forms of speech and narrative structures often differed from those of their white counterparts (Hymes, 1996). This led to African-American children's narratives not being recognized in classroom settings. Hymes argued that we do not appreciate narrative as a form of knowledge. Indeed, we under-appreciate the ways in which speech patterns are recognized in different contexts. A key concept to describe language in use is *discourse*. Hymes's work on the ethnography of communication can be linked to work by James Paul Gee on discourse and language patterns in different linguistic communities.

Theory Box: James Paul Gee on d/Discourse

James Paul Gee has worked both within the New Literacy Studies and within the ethnography of communication. Gee developed theories of language that viewed language as socially situated. Gee argued that when we try to understand a person's language-in-use, or discourse, we not only pay attention to accent, intonation and speech style of that person, among other things, but also pay attention to that person's style of clothing, gestures, and bodily movements. He calls this language-in-use discourse. When he talks about language plus other stuff he uses the term 'Discourse' (Gee, 1999b).

Hymes, Heath, Street and Gee, and many others working from socio-cultural perspectives, rendered visible issues of power within everyday meaning-making.

- What kinds of Discourses signal power?

Thinking about issues of power in relation to text perspective, purposes of texts, associated texts, practices, etc., helps readers have meta-awareness of the layered nature of literacy and meaning-making.

DISCOURSE, IDENTITY AND LITERACY

Gee's concept of **discourse** can be used with reference to a classroom. Students bring the different **Discourses** they are involved with into the classroom setting, for example, teenagers may locate their **discursive**

identity in music, clothes, ways of speaking, their artifacts, such as mobile phones, and so on. Language is rarely the only way that we display our identity. As Gee said:

> To 'pull off' being an 'X' doing 'Y' (e.g., a Los Angeles Latino street-gang member warning another gang member off his territory, or a laboratory physicist warning another laboratory physicist off her research territory) it is not enough to get just the words 'right', though that is crucial. It is necessary, as well, to get one's body, clothes, gestures, actions, interactions, ways with things, symbols, tools, technologies (be they guns or graphs), and values, attitudes, beliefs, and emotions 'right' as well, and all at the 'right' places and times. When little 'd' discourse (language-in-use) is melded integrally with non-language 'stuff' to enact specific identities and activities, then, I say that 'big D' Discourses are involved. We are all members of a many, a great many, different Discourses, Discourses which often influence each other in positive and negative ways, and which sometimes breed with each other to create new hybrids. (Gee, 1999b: 7)

This can be understood like this:

---

discourse   Language-in-use

Discourse   Language-in-use that signals membership in speech community

---

• What big 'D' discourses do you carry with you?

Literacy and learning practices are embedded in various Discourses, or ways of knowing, doing, talking, reading and writing, which are constructed and reproduced in social and cultural practice and interaction. Literacy practices are inextricably linked to oral language and how it is used. Gee's work focused on how we interact with one another, and on how the words we use are important as well as the accent, gestures, tone and body.

Discourses can represent the ways we signal our identities. Our ways of dressing, speaking, and acting all signal our membership of different identities in practice. Gee considered that people occupy different, or multiple identities, in relation to the different discourse communities we occupy. We might be a parent in one context, a teacher in another, and a member of a band in another. We can move between these identities as we go about our life. Gee, like other scholars spotlighted in the chapter, located literacy within society. He saw how literacy was shaped by how we use it. He wanted us to understand literacy as socially situated in order to foreground why school versions of literacy help some students, while hindering others. In doing so, he asked that we look at literacy and power.

Theory Box: David Barton and Mary Hamilton on local literacies

The work of Barton, Hamilton and Ivanic, and others at the University of Lancaster, has focused on how literacy practices mesh with everyday lives. In a series of studies, the socially situated nature of literacy was explored and documented. Literacy practices could be observed in communities by:

- analyzing notes taken at an allotment meeting;

- hearing about the reading of a bedtime story to a child;

- documenting the writing of letters from prison.

All of the literacy practices were associated with different domains of life, such as home, community, and classroom.

Barton and Hamilton examined the role of literacy practices and literacy events in people's lives in Lancaster. Their book, *Local Literacies*, explored the complex web of literacy practices with which people engaged. Barton and Hamilton came up with the idea of 'ruling passions' to explain how people's interests often dictated their literacy practices. These ruling passions enabled researchers to get at why literacy mattered to people, and what they used literacy for (Barton & Hamilton, 1998).

- What are your **ruling passions**? How do they shape your undersanding of literacy?

This work enables us to look at how we use literacy in everyday life, and where we can use different literacies. By associating **multiple literacies** with different domains, we can trace across a number of spaces the multiple ways literacy is used.

DIFFERENTIATING NEW LITERACY STUDIES FROM NEW LITERACIES

Given obvious and rapid changes in communication and in our ways of using communication, there have been several fields emerge within literacy education that address how we can adapt to shifts in literacy in the face of our changed **communicational landscapes**. One term that recurs in literature in the field of literacy education is 'new literacies'.

New literacies signals new kinds of texts, practices and understandings that have arisen with increased use and prevalence of technology. New literacies is a helpful way of framing literacy in the twenty-first-century.

In a handbook on new literacies, Coiro, Knobel, Lankshear and Leu (2008) identify four characteristics of new literacies research:

- New technologies offer a way to envision new literacy practices;

- New literacies are essential to economic, civic and personal participation in a world community;

- New literacies change, remix and converge as defining technologies change;

- New literacies are multimodal and multifaceted (Coiro et al., 2008).

New literacies has become a catch-all phrase for describing twenty-first-century literacy, but it should not be confused with New Literacy Studies, which has a longer tradition and which is very much a precursor to new literacies.

- What, in your view, defines the difference between new literacies and New Literacy Studies?

New Literacy Studies signals the roles of contexts and practices within contexts and the subjectivities of individuals involved in meaning-making. Building on disciplines such as anthropology, sociology, linguistics and semiotics, scholars in New Literacy Studies broadened our understandings of literacy beyond schooling. New Literacy Studies opened up a way of seeing literacy as contextualized. Through ethnographic research methods, researchers working in New Literacy Studies commit their work to a belief that literacy is best understood as a set of social practices and that there are different literacies associated with different domains of life. Literacy practices have a purpose and they are embedded in broader social and **cultural practices**. This is a distinctly different position and it should be differentiated as such.

WHY DOES LITERACY NEED THE NEW LITERACY STUDIES?

This section reflects on what these ideas can offer educators. New Literacy Studies moved literacy beyond school into different spaces, with an account of identity, and an acknowledgement of particular domains. School is just one space where literacy practices occur. However, there are other places where literacy practices have developed. In the first edition, there were a series of questions asked that are even more relevant today to educators:

- Does it help to understand how students use literacy in different domains of their lives?

- Are these forms different?

- What is the difference between image-sound texts and word-based texts?

- How often do students move from local texts to global texts?

There are certainly more questions now than there were in 2005.

Consider your students for a moment. A key aspect of your job as an educator is to teach them literacy practices.

- Do you cover all of the literacy practices that they need to survive, live, work, based on today's communicational demands?

You might notice that you have a student with a keen interest in Manga and you want to incorporate the genesis and evolution of Manga in Japan and in the West into a unit that you are doing as a part of your literacy programme. Manga is a Japanese term for comics or cartoons, which makes it an ideal genre of text to unite texts with culture and cultural practices. Part of the unit of study could involve students creating their own comics and cartoons and linking them to different cultures.

Some of the best writing is anchored in student experience and identity. Think back to Winston's eloquent narrative about contrasts between his Princeton life and the harsh realities of living in Haiti. Winston drew on his culture and his socio-economic background to express his heart-felt desire to make other students aware of racial and economic differentials of different cultures. He applied rhetorical devices and imagery to compel his reader to see his world.

- How would you introduce your literacy world to your students?

Since the first edition of *Literacy and Education*, the field has moved on with exciting work by scholars such as Hilary Janks in South Africa, who powerfully applies linguistic theory on to visual texts to demonstrate the exertion of power within texts (Janks, 2010).

The work of Kris Gutiérrez takes account of misconceptions about dual language learners and monolithic views on the literacy practices of other cultures living in the United States (Gutiérrez, 2008). Eve Gregory and

Charmian Kenner in the United Kingdom examine the importance of considering religious diversity as part of the drive to social inclusion (Gregory et al., 2007).

There is a rich repository of research on place-based education profiled in Chapter 5 by such scholars in Australia as Barbara Comber, Bill Green, and Helen Nixon (Comber et al. 2007). Catherine Compton-Lilly in the United States has followed African-American learners in Rochester, NY, over a decade, charting their literacy lives with rich ethnographic detail (Compton-Lilly, 2007). We have looked at the notion of artifactual literacy as a modern heuristic for approaching literacy in the classroom (Pahl & Rowsell, 2010). This work, separately and collectively, has moved New Literacy Studies forward into nuanced perspectives on the early work of Scribner and Cole, Shirley Brice Heath, and David Barton and Mary Hamilton.

- Who were your founding thinkers when you began as a teacher?

In this second edition of the book, we look at the New Literacy Studies five years on. In the next chapter, we look at the voluminous work in the areas of digital literacies, multimodality and multiliteracies. The focus of this chapter is research in the area of New Literacy Studies that continues to make us aware of our learners in relation to their identities, cultures, and ruling passions. New Literacy Studies continues to incorporate multiple modes of expression and communication in addition to the written word, such as drawing, talking, and texting. Literacy learners make, read, talk about, and listen to texts all of the time, and taking a New Literacy Studies approach opens up more space for learners in your classrooms.

There are new issues and different kinds of texts today than there were even five years ago. Texts are more complicated, more diffuse, and diverse. You can send emails with pictures, or upload *YouTube* videos on a teaching website while making a PowerPoint for students.

- How do you think texts have changed?

The world has moved on, but the core principles of New Literacy Studies as they were conceived in the early 1980s are alive and well.

It is still possible to observe how in ordinary life people draw on different literacy practices at different times in their lives: filling in forms, adding to a blog, sending a photograph are all part of our regular repertoires of practice. If you observe a child for any sustained period of time, you will recognize how children may make marks, play games on the computer, draw pictures, build things and this meaning-making is literacy. Some of these texts and practices you might keep and others you will throw away. In Kate's study of three London homes, 'mess' was connected with children's communicative practices: drawings and bits of writing on paper were often seen as 'stuff' to be tidied up and thrown away (Pahl, 2002).

- So, what does the New Literacy Studies offer the classroom?

The New Literacy Studies offers both a new way of looking at students, as involved in literacy in a number of different domains, and a way of seeing literacy in the classroom, as part of everyday life, meshed in with everything else. It makes the classroom both local and global.

 Activity

Using New Literacy Studies in Classrooms

At the beginning, middle, and end of the year, take an inventory of student interests and outside literacy practices. Ask students questions such as: what do you read, watch, play, and listen to outside school? You can do this as a student conference or as a questionnaire.

Access culture and cultural practice by building lessons and units around cultures and faith literacies in the classroom.

Foster an awareness of place and place-based education by conducting community walkarounds.

Make it a priority in your classroom to use different modes of expression and representation, such as analyzing photographs or illustrations, listening to songs and interpreting meanings, and reading graphic texts.

If possible, work across digital and print domains to teach lessons across the curriculum. Then, critically frame the texts that you look at in terms of format, layout, and language so that students have meta-awareness of the texts that they engage with.

Encourage modal flexibility in composition by asking students to make sound-based texts or image-based texts in addition to word-based texts.

The classroom is simply one domain where literacy occurs, but not the only one. Your classroom can reflect **local domains**: the mall, the community centre, the library; or **global domains**: the Internet, console games, popular films, raps and stories. Children's *popular culture* offers a range of ideas to link in with your students' literacy experiences out of school.

- Which artifacts are associated with local and global literacies in your classroom?

In the next section, we hone in on some of the concepts from the New Literacy Studies that might be particularly helpful.

REFLECTIONS ON LITERACY EVENTS AND LITERACY PRACTICES

In this section, we reflect once more about why the concept of literacy events and literacy practices helps us teach our students. For example, it gives you an opportunity to describe a moment when your student reads a piece of text in class as a *literacy event*. Literacy events can be found in formal and informal settings, when a student writes an essay, or when your child writes a birthday card. By putting a name on the practice, the event can be analyzed.

- What is the link between literacy events and practices?

This is worth reflecting on. While you may connect a literacy event to a classroom setting, a literacy practice is often connected to out-of-classroom settings and can be observed as a regular, iterative event. Iterative implies that something happens over and over again. Many practices have this quality: in a mosque, the same prayers are heard, in a church, the liturgy is the same every week. Many families have things they do on a regular basis, and literacy practices fit into this: thank-you letters to relatives, or e-cards to friends and family. We can hold a literacy practice in our heads from one day to the next. The practice of filling in a form can be drawn upon when filling in a new form. Thinking about literacy as situated in **autonomous** and ideological models of literacy is explained below.

> We take the concepts of 'autonomous models of literacy' and 'ideological models of literacy' from Brian Street (1995). He saw the words as meaning:
>
> | Autonomous | Ideological |
> | --- | --- |
> | Literacy as a separate 'thing', as a set of skills | Literacy as connected with cultural and social practices in the world |

- When would you identify autonomous models and literacy and when would you understand literacy to be ideologically situated?

CRITICAL LITERACY AND THE NEW LITERACY STUDIES

With strong ties to New Literacy Studies, **critical literacy** has been an emerging conceptual framework for literacy scholars. Researchers engaged at grassroots levels in out-of-school contexts with students who experience marginalization and disempowerment in many areas of their lives take a critical literacy approach to research, theory and practice. Recent international studies, featured in Chapter 6, have focused on critical literacy in the context of post-apartheid South Africa (Janks, 2010), and critical multiliteracies in relation to place and space in the context of climate change in Australia (Comber, 2010).

Scholars using critical literacy **pedagogy** have interrogated texts as sites of power imbalances. As educators, you can combine the principles of New Literacy Studies with critical literacy by adopting such text analyses models as Janks' Power, Access, Diversity, and Design model, which unveils and interrogates hidden ideologies and discourses in texts (Janks, 2010). This approach draws on previous research that also studied texts as ideologically situated and therefore capable of being broken apart. Muspratt, Luke and Freebody (1997), in their four resources model, showed how this could be done with a focus on texts as a source of power, and provided a methodology for interrogating texts that uncovered the processes and practices of ideologies within discourses. Rogers and colleagues (Rogers et al., 2009) have shown that a focus on critical inquiry and analysis creates a problem-solving, inclusive space within classrooms and communities that can shift and sustain change. In Rogers' work, she focuses on the notion of *teacher inquiry*, whereby a circle of change, involving questioning, considering data, and then creating new kinds of questions, can emerge (Rogers et al., 2009).

- What kind of questions would you want to engage with in your classroom?

ECOLOGICAL APPROACHES TO LITERACY

In an effort to link data collection and analysis to neighbourhoods and communities, several researchers who work within New Literacy Studies and related fields have adopted **ecological** approaches to theorize the relationship between home and school, for instance, as interconnected systems. Neuman and Celano (2001) conducted a comparative study of four neighbourhoods in Philadelphia in terms of the opportunities that they offered for children and their families to engage in literacy-related activities. They argue that 'learning and development cannot be considered apart from the individual's social environment, the ecological niche' (Neuman & Celano, 2001: 8). Their method involved walking through a block of each neighbourhood and systematically noting:

- every store and stand likely to sell reading materials;

- every **sign** and its condition (readability);

- public spaces where reading could be undertaken;

- relevant institutional sites (libraries, child care centres, etc.).

They found that neighbourhoods of different socio-economic status showed 'major and striking differences at almost all levels' in terms of access to literacy resources and opportunities (Neuman & Celano, 2001: 15).

- What are the resources for literacy in your community?

Scholars working in the New Literacy Studies examined the local and the situated literacies of people living in particular communities, but what has been less explored is how the local and local hubs co-exist as networks of influence on people in different circumstances. Relatively few studies have focused on the nuances of varied contexts and the relationship of community sites to each other. Future directions in New Literacy Studies will lead to more studies that examine ecological dimensions of communities as geographies of opportunities or misfortunes.

Theory Box: Sue Nichols on capturing children's artifacts through multimodal literacies

The 'Changing Lives' project invited children in Years 1 to 6 to become family and self-historians and to 'catch' what they had found through using multiple modalities. The project was designed to be inclusive of children's diverse cultural resources, adaptable to their ages and abilities, and connectable with different curriculum areas. The Year 1 class focused on exploring the very beginning of their lives – their birth and infancy.

In the first session, the author told the children a story from her own life. She recalled how at the age of four, she had been invited to choose just one toy to take with her on a long journey to a new country. This introduced two key ideas: that our life pathways can take us to different places and that objects may take on special meanings. In the discussion that followed, children were asked if they knew where they had been born. This discussion was inclusive of local as well as more distant places with care taken not to communicate value for one over the other. Children were invited to take the conversation home in three ways:

- To talk with family members about the circumstances of their birth;

- To borrow family photos;

- To select a special object which had been in their possession from their early years to bring in to school.

These materials were worked on in several ways but one activity stands out as particularly generative for engaging young children in the process of producing multimodal texts. Using an ordinary digital camera, a cheap tripod, and a classroom table covered and backed with sheets of blue cardboard, a photo studio was set up in the classroom. Each child had brought in a special object and they took it in turns to pose their object (mostly soft toys) in front of the camera, coming back behind the camera to check on the view.

Talk between the author and each child focused on design choices for composing an image, with options including the degree of close-up, lighting, angle and the way the object was placed. Some children were quite particular about the features of their object that they wanted to highlight in the composition of the image. One boy had brought in a plush toy shark and stated that he wanted it to 'look scary'; he was assisted to prop the shark with its mouth facing the camera and to take the zoom in close.

At the next session, children were encouraged to add linguistic text to the images of their significant objects through one or more of three options: speech bubble, thought bubble and caption. Beforehand, the author had copied each image into a PowerPoint slide; in this programme, bubbles are 'callouts' and are accessed through the shapes menu, while captions can be made by inserting a text box. Several children chose to comment on the circumstances of their toy's unusual visit to the classroom, e.g., 'Beafo is very shy. It is her first time to go out' or in a thought bubble 'Where am I?' There were narrative elements in some captions, as in the case of when a boy attributed his car with an exciting back-story: 'My car knows everything about the world. My car has been all over the world'. It was interesting to see some children describe the qualities of their toy in a thought bubble (e.g., 'I think I am cute and snugly') rather than in a caption (e.g., 'My toy is cute and snugly'). This design choice highlights the toy's status as a character rather than a mere object.

The PowerPoint became a class text that expressed, through the use of artifacts, images, linguistic text and digital design elements, a significant aspect of their young lives. It was displayed at the school's 'Art Night' and attracted considerable attention from the children and their family members.

- Can you think of a valued artifact that you could bring to a group situation and talk about?

CONCLUSION

Literacy is bound up with our identity and our practices. The shaping of our literacy practices takes place in a number of different domains, for example, home, school, and workplace. Taking on an approach that looks at literacy as a social practice involves a number of key thoughts. It involves acknowledging that school is only *one setting* where literacy takes place. It recognizes that the resources used to teach in classrooms might be different from the resources used by students in their homes. To conclude the chapter, New Literacy Studies research has widened its scope to examine and critically frame the nuances of power within communities, to document ecological aspects of the local and differentials in access to resources in communities, to understand specific sites in the local, such as churches, libraries and malls, and to expand our understanding of texts beyond the written word.

READING THIS BOOK

As you read this book you will note that there are repetitions. We have deliberately returned to concepts that we consider central to contemporary understandings of New Literacy Studies in the classroom:

- Literacy as material;

- Literacy as social practice;

- The integral role of culture, community and identity;

- Literacy and space;

- Literacy and time;

- Multimodal literacies.

Reading this book becomes a spiral process by which concepts are elaborated on and their different facets explored in each individual chapter. **We then tie these ideas together in our final chapter on curriculum and pedagogy.**

2

Multimodal literacies: New ways of reading and writing

Figure 2.1 Dionne's Manga character

A MEANING MAKER REPRESENTS HER WORLD MULTIMODALLY

Dionne and her friend Bonni have been making scrapbooks to represent their home literacy practices. This was as part of a project called 'Writing in the Home and in the Street'. One day, I (Kate) came into the library where we met weekly to discuss the girls' scrapbooks and review the images. Dionne showed me a new page of her book. She had been documenting her home writing practices in different ways. She had pasted in bus tickets to represent her home/school journeys. She also had been representing her online and offline literacy practices. She did this by cutting and pasting an image of the 'Google' search engine, with the open box in the middle of the page. Then she pasted what she had been looking for on the search engines, which in this case was an example of a Manga drawing. She hand-drew her own Manga drawing, in order to signal what she meant by Manga. Dionne had therefore represented the search engine (Google) by cutting and pasting from a screen shot of Google together with a hand-drawn Manga person, and had also pasted in her bus tickets. Dionne's meaning-making was entirely multimodal, being composed of cut-out screen shots, bus tickets collected and pasted in, and hand-drawing. In this way, she could make meaning from an ensemble of semiotic resources and reassemble them to create a new text signalling her home writing practices.

 Key themes in the chapter:

- Contemporary multimodality
- Materiality
- Affordances and constraints
- Synaesthesia
- Texts as traces of practice
- Reading path
- Digital literacies
- Artifactual literacies
- Critically framing multimodality

INTRODUCTION

Imagine that you are sitting in a café with your laptop doing a web search, looking up occasionally at a painting on the wall. While you find an address on *Google Maps*, someone sits next to you texting a friend on their iPhone. You are aware of the brushstrokes in the painting as much as you are aware of the feverish pace of your neighbour's typing. This is a fairly common sight. This moment in time typifies what our communicational landscape looks like. Scrolling, tapping, sliding, clicking, repertoires of practice and accompanying texts keep changing and we keep adapting to them with little question and little pause. Changes in how we communicate and compose texts keep shifting as we continue to expand and stretch our capacities to take them up. Today we have 3-D, immersive, material, artifactual worlds that sit quietly among digital worlds and our students exist among them.

- How can we possibly build our teaching around such variegated places and spaces?

WHAT IS OUR WORLD TODAY?

The students that we teach are and have been in contact with this world of new technologies, three-dimensionality, videogames, screens and mobile devices for some time. They live in local spaces, filled with global advertising and a plethora of images. In this chapter, we offer frameworks, theories and applications for thinking about ways of negotiating your teaching of literacy with multimodalities. Here are some questions to think about as educators of twenty-first-century learners:

- How can I teach students about modes and the potential of certain modes at particular moments?

This question is about whether to use a video or a PowerPoint or a piece of written text to convey a particular message (e.g., which **mode** to choose).

- How can I mediate or reconcile modes and **modal learning** with curricular imperatives and objectives?

This question is about recognizing that students have a felt connection to certain modes over other modes (e.g., creating a script instead of a written text). Modal learning is about accessing their natural modal choices with more scripted modal choices.

- How does my teaching need to change so that I balance multimodality with skills teaching?

This question is about embedding literacy learning in a multimodal format (e.g., encouraging the use of explanatory writing for a videogame).

- What does multimodality do to more traditional concepts, such as reading and writing?

This question is about what the image or gesture will bring to the meaning.

It helps to consider the types of texts that our students use, which are relevant to literacy teaching. These include both online and offline texts.

This chapter explores new ways of seeing texts. In this chapter, we draw on Gee's concept of big and little 'D' discourses (Gee, 1999b). These are ways of speaking, behaving, acting in culturally-specific ways, as described in Chapter 1. Texts are seen as carrying different Discourses, as made up of visuals, sounds, movements and gestures. Texts can be seen as artifacts that trace back to people and places.

- Take an online or offline text that you are currently reading, and consider that this book or text contains a history of its production.

Texts contain echoes of other texts and other communicative artifacts. A text will feel a certain way and have a certain font, format and cover. These decisions reflect choices that someone has made about content and how design has an important part to play in the message of the text. A different modality opens up when you introduce other modes (e.g., including visuals into reports). In Chapter 5, we talk about this as the notion of 'sedimented identities in texts', which is the idea that meaning makers, whether singly or collectively, sediment parts of themselves into texts (Rowsell & Pahl, 2007). In this chapter, we look at identity in terms of how learners use the principles and practices of multimodality when they make meaning with texts across a variety of contexts.

MULTIMODALITY: AN OVERVIEW

Multimodality is a field that takes account of how individuals make meaning with different kinds of modes. The shift from written to visual texts in contemporary culture means that a focus on semiotics, the study of signs, is important (Kress & Van Leeuwen, 1996). There has been so much dynamic research on multimodality over the past decade (Lancaster, 2003; Walsh, 2003; Siegal, 2006; Stein, 2007; Jewitt, 2009; Vasudevan, 2009; Wohlwend, 2009; Kress, 2010; Pahl & Rowsell, 2010). We also highlight Gunther Kress's book, *Before Writing*. The book maps out a language and logic of multimodality entirely premised on how children make meaning in the world: through senses, gut instincts, improvisations, and fearless creativity. In his eloquent words, 'we cannot understand how children find their way into print unless we understand the principles of their meaning making' (Kress, 1997: xvii). In this chapter, we build on this work.

Multimodal research unveils aspects of English and literacy that have been held back by a linguistic analysis. Take the research of Pippa Stein and her work with young children and their multimodal meaning-making and transformation of ideas into hand-made artifacts (Stein, 2007). Or the work of Kate Pahl (2004), who connects the sign to the sign-maker by tracing subjectivities embedded into texts. Or Carey Jewitt's detailed work analyzing diagrams of scientific processes in science class (2009) as preferred ways of understanding material. Or Charmian Kenner's (2004) interpretation of spatial organization and the framing of writing on the page, its directionality, the angle of its scripts, and the shape and size of script. These studies, individually and collectively, redress an over-emphasis in the past on the written word.

- Take a piece of writing that you have completed and locate the history of its making, connecting it to moments when you felt strongly or less strongly about how the text was produced and designed (e.g., a reflective piece of writing).

When teachers work with children today, they have to navigate increased testing regimes. For example, students have to perform end-of-year tests based on knowledge of literature. These are often founded on autonomous views of literacy, that is, literacy as a set of skills. Outside school, literacy is linked to design, to presentation and to form. Teachers have to think about how these forms manifest in the classroom. Often these out-of-school literacies are not allowed into the classroom. Sites such as *Facebook* are banned by schools.

- How can teachers make sense of these two very different ways of seeing literacy; one is about the written word on the page, the other is about the design of a series of different visual signs on a screen?

In this chapter, we argue that both forms of literacy need to be present in the classroom. There are ways of finding space for multimodality while at the same time fulfilling objectives and preparing for curricular demands. Modal learning (Rowsell, forthcoming), or teaching through the lens and properties of modes, is one way of lifting out the traditional, skills-based model and merging it with the new and multimodal. Focusing on one mode (e.g., the visual) or combined modes (e.g., visual plus audio) can help students to replicate production practices as they are lived, used and understood in the workplace, in the home and on the street.

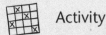 Activity

Teaching through Modes

Think about your students, whether primary, middle, secondary, or adult. Now think about a targeted skill such as persuasive writing on a topic like sustainability or eco-systems. Start the lesson with a slideshow of connected and contrastive images depicting sustainability: a tsunami, a littered cityscape, a green building, a garden, human consumption, compost, a bird in oil, etc.

- Which images call up sustainable practices?

- Which images call up global warming?

Students can then assess these images for themselves. Images that are consonant and disconsonant with sustainability compel students to visualize their persuasive argument.

Then play three scenes from the film *Avatar* that consider sustainable issues in Pandora, the place where the *Nav'i* live. After watching the three clips, ask students to write a paragraph in the voice of a character in the movie.

Teachers can even extend the lesson by showing the documentary *Wasteland*, which presents a famous Brazilian artist who moved to Rio de Janeiro to build installations out of garbage with homeless people. Such an extension on the theme of sustainability imbues a sense of community, of taking care of our local worlds.

Finish the lesson materializing the concept through an activity where the students use arts and crafts to create a sustainable invention out of materials. These can be brought in and include artifacts that are recyclable, such as boxes, newsprint, cups, etc. The lesson teaches students to visualize concepts, to write prose based on moving images, and to use materials to create an object. This object will then represent and articulate the idea of sustainability.

THE MOTIVATED SIGN

A main characteristic of multimodal texts are that they are designed in certain ways. As educators, we should interrogate the choices made in the creation of texts. That is, texts carry the motivations of the producer (e.g., child, songwriter, publisher, poet, etc.), or as Kress expresses it, texts are *motivated signs* (Kress, 1997).

- How do texts signal the motivations of the producer?

Kress speaks of 'best ways' of representing meanings. In some circumstances, meanings are best expressed through words and pictures, whereas in others, movement or three dimensions might be preferable. Children's artifacts carry with them the choices they made during the process – why they opted for red sweeps of colour with a bit of green versus purple sweeps of colour with a bit of green.

AFFORDANCES AND CONSTRAINTS

Often the issue of materiality comes down to the **affordances** and **constraints** of the materials that we use. Affordances are the possibilities that a particular form offers a text-maker. Kress asks: what are the affordances of a mode and what are its constraints?

- What materials give a text greater power and attention and what materials lessen its power and attention?

In writing an essay, a student strives to have an academic voice, a demonstration of research skills, a use of proper and accurate grammar, punctuation and mechanics, and an understanding of style. Understanding and applying the principles of academic writing *affords* opportunities to succeed in school, whereas not accounting for punctuation – vocabulary – structure *constrains* success in academic writing.

When students create a PowerPoint presentation to show, or make a film out of Movie Maker, they have to consider font, use of graphics, amount of written text, summarizing and selecting key points, and on the whole, take account of the *affordances* of text features when creating their presentation. As sign-makers, students have to factor in the benefit of each material they use. The possibilities open to the student, and the choices they make, in relation to the affordance of each mode, have yet to be subject to an assessment regime, but questions of assessment of multimodal choice remain pertinent in our multimodal world.

For every text there are alternative choices in form and function. Given the sheer number of texts today, there is ample choice and variety in what form best suits content. As a teacher, it makes our jobs more difficult because some lessons might better suit a digital medium or more differentiated activity, whereas with others, a traditional lecture format best suits instruction. Equally, when assigning tasks, students today need variety in the forms and functions of texts. If a topic demands peer-to-peer learning, then there needs to be more group work and you want to avoid a lecture format; perhaps you can skype an expert somewhere in the world. There are moments when a style of teaching and learning might demand social networking. If, however, the topic demands more meaning than others then as literacy teachers we need flexibility in repertoires and tools that we use to plan and assess lessons and student performance.

- What are your modal choices when teaching and why?

SYNAESTHESIA

Children are guided far more by what Kress refers to as *synaesthetic activities*. They are not as influenced as adults are by the predominance of written text, and tend to be guided more by other modes, such as the visual, kinesthetic, three-dimensional and gestural modes. They draw on these different modes freely when making meaning, and may not see one as more salient than another. Instead, children may choose the most appropriate mode for their meaning-making activities.

Vignette: Synaesthetic responses to children's illustrations

By Candace Kuby

In Candace Kuby's primary classroom in the Southern United States, 5- and 6-year-olds used painting as a way to process racial bus segregation. She wanted her students to tease apart the multiple, complex voices of segregation so decided to create a learning engagement around the post-modern picture book, *Voices in the Park* (Browne, 2001). The book is divided into four sections, or voices of gorillas, each telling their perspective of visiting a park. Candace explained to her students that they would use the text structure of Browne's book to write their own story about the day Rosa Parks, an African-American, was arrested on a bus in Alabama. The students were divided into four voices (groups): Rosa Parks, the White bus driver, the other African-Americans, and the other White people.

As Candace looked at the students' illustrations, she began to experience a range of emotions. Using the notion of synaesthesia helped her to unpack each image. Synaesthesia literally means 'join' and 'senses'. Traditionally, we think of synaesthesia as a term to describe an artist who experiences the world using more than one sense at a time (a musician that sees a particular colour when they hear a musical note). Candace uses the concept of synaesthesia to refer to the multiple senses evoked in the viewer. Approaching art in this way 'means not looking at what art is, but at what it does, or its effects' (Kind, 2010: 127–128). Candace asked herself questions such as: What emotions and senses are evoked from viewing this image? How do aspects of the illustrations (i.e., colour, lines, size, positionality) stir up multiple senses?

Hunter authored a page for the portion of the book from the perspective of the White bus driver. The text for the page he illustrated said, 'I looked around and saw that other Black people had sad faces because Rosa was getting arrested' (Figure 2.2). Hunter drew four people brown (African-Americans) with what appeared to be streams of tears falling to the ground. The fifth person, much smaller in size, was colored yellow with a blue hat, which is assumed to be the bus driver. Hunter also used speech bubbles to capture the voices of the African-American people such as 'sad' and 'waaay' (sound of crying).

Several aspects from Hunter's illustration evoked a synaesthetic response. Candace was drawn to the large, numerous tears falling and the distinct frowns on the faces of the African-Americans. The combination of the frowns pointing down and the tears streaming to the ground, took her eyes to the bottom of the image. This evoked a heavy sadness and stirred up anger because of the oppression African-Americans experienced. The use of speech bubbles with words such as 'sad' and 'waaay', combined with the tears, evoked empathy. A viewer can smell the saltiness and moisture from the tears, can feel the tears rolling down the faces, and hear shouts of frustration. Using the notion of synaesthesia allows a person to embrace multiple senses when looking at artistic responses. It also invites the viewer to think beyond representation and instead imagine art as a place of encounter.

Figure 2.2   Hunter's synaesthetic response

In many ways, the notion of **synaesthesia** is much like our notion of creativity and creative expression. Creativity and synaesthesia rely on all of the senses when we make meaning. The artifacts we make reflect synaesthetic activity by being composed of sound, of materials, of words, etc. In early years settings, creativity is in full bloom in the types of texts used and the materials used to create them. Young children move quite naturally across modes and their use of modes such as colour and brush stroke can signal an emotion or feeling.

As our schooling progresses into the junior and intermediate years, creative expression or synaesthetic activity changes, and there is far more of a focus on writing *and* skills acquisition. Once children enter school, there is a privileging of the written over other modes. Schooled literacy focuses on written language above and beyond other, alternative modes.

- How do students engage with the multimodal in their out-of-school textual productions?

MATERIALITY OF TEXTS

In *Before Writing* (1997), Kress asks an important question which is salient today given all of the shifts in reading and writing practices:

- What kind of reader do we want to produce and for what and whose ends?

The question is polemical in that we all must read and write in certain ways to work and fulfil daily lives. However, at the same time, the question is central when educating school children. This question takes account of the different texts the children we teach encounter in their daily lives.

Our understanding of texts, on content, structural and visual levels, guides the way we read and produce future texts. We learn about writing from our past experiences as a reader and a writer. These past experiences guide our writing. When we write a piece of fiction, we draw on our experiences of stories. We cobble together our conception of writing within a genre by reading other texts within that genre.

Similarly, children who watch animated movies like *Shrek* or *Dora the Explorer* incorporate phrases from these movies into their own speech. Children often acquire idioms and turns of phrase in their viewing of videos or DVDs. By extension, Gee argues that children actually think and use language in different, more complex ways by using videogames.

Theory Box: James Paul Gee on meaning-making and videogames

James Paul Gee (2003), claims that in the 'space' or use of videogames there is an interweaving of plot, characterization, practice (e.g., actions used to fight off evil and promote good), and elaborate problem-solving. Children experiment within this forum by taking on new identities and understanding the nature of new cultures. The key to succeeding within the world of computer games is understanding the culture and idiosyncrasies and dispositions of the characters.

Gee highlights important skills students acquire in their use of videogames:

- active and critical thinking;

- an appreciation and understanding of design;

- problem-solving skills;

- principles of semiotics (as in images working with words, with actions, with symbols, with artifacts);

- identity principles in taking on different personalities and working within their logic;

- an understanding of what it means to work within cultural models (i.e., models carrying values, beliefs, etc.).

When you start to play a videogame, your experience is embodied and guided by these principles.

- What are the teachable moments within a videogame?

Theory Box: Sandra Schamroth-Abrams on videogaming and education – key elements that foster active learning and critical thinking

'In gaming, you get to choose what happens. And like more so than in a choose-your-own-adventure book. [When] gaming, you get to get more than two options or three options. You get lots of crisscrossing options. But even in Mario you could choose to go to one door or the other door. You get to go back to the other door later.'

–David, 8th Grader

(Cont'd)

'When I play videogames like I kind of figure out like what to do ... I don't read the manuals. Like it kind of just comes to me.'

–Lyle, 7th Grader

'Learning in school is kind of boring ... because ... it's just been 50 minutes of someone talking to me about something ... but learning with video-games you actually get to try it out like hands on sort of.'

–James, 6th Grader

When middle school gamers, David, Lyle, and James spoke about their literacy activities, they called attention to the ways videogaming practices are recursive, agentive, and intuitive. Each expressed the ability to control the trajectory of his gaming and the enjoyment of exploring in a virtual arena. In so doing, the three boys highlighted the discrepancies between the transmission model of learning (e.g., '50 minutes of someone talking to me about something') and the Deweyean concept of 'learning by doing', suggesting that out-of-school multimodal activities, such as vide-ogaming, place the students at the center of their meaning-making, offer students attempts to rethink their choices, and enable students to learn from others.

It is well known that videogames help players hone critical thinking skills and foster practice and experimentation and the discussion of game play and the collaboration within game play are key components to belonging to that particular videogame community. Often I have seen gamers, like Lyle, who won't read manuals but who will learn how to play not only by experimenting with the game, but also by speaking with other gamers and learning from 'cheats' posted by other gamers on game websites. In other words, the gaming community privileges knowledge sharing because it is a practice that supports a learning process manifested in improved game play and mastery of skills. Outside school, students may be developing funds of knowledge that are specific to the digital age – skills and knowl-edge that privilege autonomous discovery, recursive learning, and collabo-rative practices.

Gaming and school?

Though commercial videogames may not make their ways into classrooms because of curricular constraints and financial limitations, educators can build upon the skills students develop as they interact with multimodalities on and off the screen. As David noted above, gaming provided him 'lots of crisscrossing options', and contemporary education needs to offer students interconnected options be they with texts, practices, and/or class structure. Students need to see that in school they can return to their work as a means to explore new meanings without consequence. In other words, though revising a paper, a problem, or a stance may be recursive in nature, students need more freedom to move in and out of texts to see how their choices impact their understandings. There needs to be room for students to take control of their learning and partake in collaborative explorations and knowledge sharing (as opposed to being provided the information); with a more agentive stance in the classrooms, students will have opportunities to embrace recursive learning and grow, not suffer, from their mistakes.

WORKING WITH STUFF

It is the *manner* in which we make texts that signifies our own interpretation. It is, as Kress puts it, the *stuff* we use to make texts which inscribes our identities into them (Kress, 1997). *Stuff* can range from different fonts, to high-quality paper, to cut-out bits of paper glued on to cardboard, to a child's drawing – any material that best suits a text based on the *interest* of the producer. Kress uses the term **materiality** to describe the stuff we use to make a text. Stuff could consist of words and our knowledge of action and gesture in role-play or visuals and written words combined with our knowledge of characterization and plot in writing a story for class. Importantly, Kress discusses meaning-as-form and form-as-meaning. You cannot have one without the other, and when we create texts, meaning and form stand on equal footing.

 Activity

Questions to consider with children's writing:

- In which genre are they working?
- What is the function of the text?
- What language or Discourse should they use?
- How much of their identities, for example, out-of-school interests, should a child bring to a text?
- Who is the intended audience?
- What is the format and layout of the text?
- Where will the text be read?
- Is the text represented best in print or electronic form?
- Are the visuals realistic or interpretative?
- Should they include photographs or illustrations?
- Should the text be viewed in one, two or three dimensions?

More than ever, the materials we use to make texts are key to under-standing texts. A child creating a web page considers what links there will be to other pages; she considers the amount and placement of writ-ten text; she considers the colour scheme and the purpose of visuals in the interface; she decides whether to include movement by using *Flash* or other programs; she decides whether to include sound; she considers the size of the monitor on which the text will be viewed. Collectively, these decisions comprise the materiality of the text and they have everything to do with how we make meaning from a text. We have more choices than ever in our making and reading of texts, which implies that, more than ever, we have to understand and interpret the material-ity of texts. In teaching, there is a difference between lecturing with or without overheads versus teaching using PowerPoint. The former teach-ing method is still an accepted model, but perhaps less stimulating com-pared to the interactive, visual and audio-driven nature of Prezi.

TEXTS AS TRACES OF PRACTICE

Consider for a moment the texts that you use in your classroom. In all likelihood the types of texts you will see are textbooks in various subject areas; reading centres with picture books or novels, non-fiction texts, perhaps dual language and community language texts; policy docu-ments such as curriculum documents, special needs and English as an Additional Language (ELL) documents, school policies; posters, maps, student artifacts; binders filled with evaluation forms, assessment tools, etc. These texts are not only **traces** of the culture in which you work, traces of you as a teacher with your notion of pedagogy and practice, but also traces of various other contexts all sitting within one room with 20 to 30 students. As discussed and illustrated above, texts are traces of people, contexts and implied practices.

- What practices can you find hidden within the texts within your classroom?

When you use a reading scheme it carries within it a specific model of literacy, a specific method of teaching (e.g., direct and structured versus more informal), specific literacy practices, such as guided reading or lit-erature circles, and sometimes even specific readers in mind (e.g., an ELL emphasis in a reading scheme).

Textbooks are the product of a long collaborative process among pub-lishing teams that bring their own identities and context agendas into books that ultimately guide our understandings of how to teach a discipline. A reading scheme carries ways of teaching, philosophies of literacy, *and* literacy practices that should take place – even *where* they should take place (e.g., in small groups with different worksheets that students complete at a table). While these practices are taken for granted in classrooms, reading scheme books assume and reflect these practices. The reading scheme book is a text which retains traces of its making, and the identities of the makers are inscribed within the text.

 Activity

Tracing Practices in Your Classroom

Take out a reading scheme book or textbook you use in your classroom.

Take a look at the student book and the teacher's resource book.

Answer all or some of these questions:

- Who is the author?
- Who is the publisher?
- Can you identify a model of teaching and learning?
- How would you use this resource?
- How does it inform or guide your teaching?
- Does it provide modifications for other student learners?
- What is the design of the text?
- How does the visual work with the written?
- Write a synopsis of how you might use the textbook and some of the practices that would grow out of using it.
- Describe how you might design the textbook or teacher's resource book differently.

One thing to consider is students' use of academic literacies in different domains.

- Can you think of an instance when the multimodal can be used with academic literacy, for example, a voice-over to a film?

Theory Box: Gunther Kress and Theo Van Leeuwen on the grammar of visual design

Gunther Kress and Theo Van Leeuwen, in *Reading Images: The Grammar of Visual Design* (1996), demonstrate that visual text has a grammar of its own which can work in sync and at odds with written text. An example in speech that Kress and Van Leeuwen supply is a child saying 'This is a heavy hill'. Although the child is constrained by not having the word 'steep', he focuses on particular aspects of climbing a hill and uses an available form to do so. A child uses available resources, as they put it, to make a text or express a thought. The basis of this thought comes from experiences with texts and speech they have acquired and stored away. They focus on the 'interest' of the sign-maker as pivotal in creating the text (Kress & Van Leeuwen, 1996).

- Can you think of a way of describing your students' visual capabilities?

Theory Box: Some key principles

There are key principles we think about in our making and reading of texts:

- The idea behind the text (e.g., a manual explaining how a washing machine works);

- The relationship with the viewer (e.g., a consumer with a warranty who wants to know the parts or be able to fix the machine);

- What the genre demands of the text (e.g., active verbs and paragraphs with lots of visuals to support written texts and phone numbers in case they cannot sort out the problem).

Kress and Van Leeuwen offer a grammar of visual design to demonstrate that the visual is (often) a separate medium of expression with its own rules and conventions. They address a variety of texts from children's picture books to social studies textbooks to advertisements to works of art to sculpture. Kress and Van Leeuwen provide a framework for visual analysis that we can use to interpret texts (Kress & Van Leeuwen, 1996).

One of the most powerful vehicles for the visual is to establish a relationship between the producer and the reader. They discuss how producers are cognizant and write for and to a model reader through their choices in language and in multimodality.

Over the course of an interview with a senior editor at Ginn Publishers in the United Kingdom, the interviewee discussed the role of **visual communication** in children's books. When asked about the role of the visual, the interviewee maintained:

> The visual has an increasingly important role. We are increasingly putting more emphasis into things like typography. Typography is something you have to get right with big books. ... We spend a lot of time briefing artists on what texts should look like. We stress the sort of detail that can get missed, like we do not want kids in the books to be in spotless clothing all of the time ... . (Rowsell, 2000)

Clearly, in light of new technologies, there is a greater consciousness of the visual as carrying its own informational and ideological potential.

 Activity

The Grammar of Visual Design

Think about the list of key principles to consider when 'reading' an image. In the UK, a booklet, *More than Just Words: Multimodal Texts in the Classroom* invites teachers to focus on the following questions when looking at children's multimodal texts:

- How can we describe what children know and can do as shown in their multimodal texts – in this case drawing plus writing?

- What are the implications for classroom practice: how can teachers help pupils develop and extend their control of different modes (QCA, 2004)?

The booklet highlighted how children's choices about layout features, such as colour, font size and style, choice of language and overall design in combining words and images, all worked to create different ways in which the texts were read and received (QCA, 2004).

The booklet left teachers with the question:

- What does getting better at multimodal presentation look like?

- How would you assess multimodality in the classroom?

READING PATH

Texts are no longer straightforward. Electronic texts do not follow a linear path, but instead follow a series of links that lead you into different texts tied but separate from the original one. Take a typical web page. Written parts of the text are often labels for an image or instructions. It is often said that the upper left-hand corner of a text has the most important information, as opposed to the bottom right-hand corner.

Sometimes there are sound bytes, there is movement in animated text, there are captions at the bottom related to the text but somewhat outside it, there are hotspots taking us to another site or another page, there is hypertext giving definitions, and so on. All of these bits of text move us around the page and we have far more options than we did before. With these texts in mind, we need to re-evaluate our notion of *reading path*.

- Go onto a website and evaluate it with these principles in mind.

Theory Box: Gunther Kress and Carey Jewitt on revising our notion of reading path

Carey Jewitt and Gunther Kress argue that we must attend to the role of new technologies because they are demanding different kinds of skills from our students. They claim that these new forms of communication carry modes, which are at one and the same time visual, tactile, linguistic, graphic, and that these modes carry meanings in the texts. New communicational practices involve image, gesture, movement, music, speech and sound-effect. Where in the past, students read a text and although they could look ahead to what will be said or unfold, they followed a standard path. Such is not the case with modern texts. With modern texts, readers move around to different texts, with less of a sustained linear reading path, encompassing a wider set of genres of text (Jewitt & Kress, 2003).

Different cultures have made decisions about reading paths in their writing systems, whether from right to left or from left to right. Multimodal texts open up the question again by allowing the user to choose where you go in a text. With the predominance of technology, computer screens and images frame our use of language. In this way, writing, where it occurs on screen, is subordinated to the logic of the screen (Kress, 2010). We are far more likely to be aware of headers and footers, of boldface text, and of double- versus single-spaced writing on screen compared to hand-written text. We have a visual reflex when we write on screen.

- Think about an online and offline text you have just read, how was the reading experience different?

Reading paths on screen are not necessarily governed by the whims of the reader, but instead, as frequent users of electronic texts we are socialized into ways or practices of using these texts. Students we teach learn how to move around web pages and use hypertext when they need to by observing others, and by experimenting with new media themselves. Students have been socialized into the world of contemporary media. They are far more disposed to seeing the screen as a point of reference for **strategies** of reading. In this way, literacy skills are tied to reading strategies used during computer use (e.g., cutting and pasting text, using spell and grammar check, formatting texts). These practices are natural, assumed and tacit.

 Activity

Reading Path

Get on the web and visit three websites.

Chart how you navigate through them.

Write down your path and where it led you.

Then look at a web page in greater detail.

Analyze where written text sits and where the visuals are.

What is the logic behind your reading path?

What compelled you to move to another page and did you return to the original one?

MULTIMODALITY … FIVE YEARS ON

Here, we take stock of all of the new genres of text in the world. Indeed, there are so many more texts that did not exist five years ago when we wrote the first edition. Different Apps, social media, wearable devices keep evolving that continue to call into question what we mean by the term 'text'. In teaching students today, we must ensure that we keep, even somewhat, apace with changes in the form and function of texts. In this way, multimodality and its nature has also moved on. As educators, in the main, we accept that texts are as visual as they are written. We acknowledge that writing often implies skills beyond word-smithing and crafting a sentence. It is still helpful to view **texts as artifacts** and as comprised of modes. Texts signal intended practices and how producers intend a text to be used (e.g., at home, at school, in groups, etc.). But, in what ways has multimodality moved on?

In terms of reading, through the work of scholars such as Alyson Simpson (Walsh & Simpson, 2010) and Maureen Walsh (Walsh, 2011), we know that the nature of 'reading' has changed in multimodal times. Technical skills such as browsing screens, scrolling through text or clicking on hyperlinks, communicating through social networks to share, acquire and communicate information, using converged technologies such as phones that are cameras are skills that are multimodal practices that we could not have predicted in 2005. The pervasiveness of touch screens which you slide and tap were in their infancy and still are, in many ways, in terms of their implications for decoding and comprehending texts.

- How do these skills and devices impact how we are teaching reading in our classrooms?

When graphic and digital texts contain images, hypertext, sound and moving images, how do these modes of meaning impact the reading process? How does a reader 'read' a visual or sound accompanied with print? Reading a word and reading a word with visuals and sounds are different acts of comprehension. Given the pervasive nature of multimodal texts, how can teachers be explicitly taught how to move from the word to the image? Or, how do learners develop language and metacognitive processes for differentiating between word-based, linguistic texts and image-based, multimodal texts. Reading implies the skills of decoding words, but it also involves using visuals to comprehend texts, using spatial dimensions to problem-solve in spaces.

 Activity

Word Study on Tablets

To complete this assignment in K-3 classrooms, a teacher needs five tablets with four students at each station. Students will rotate in their groups to five different tablet stations:

- letter patterns;
- sound patterns;
- cloze activities;
- spatial games;
- wiki texts.

The first station focuses on combining letters to make words by combining a list of letters into as many words as you can make in two minutes. The second station hones sound-based skills and phonological awareness by asking students to match sounds such as long i or gh with matching sounds such as time-spine and rough-stuff.

The third station asks students to contextualize words within narratives to develop comprehension of larger blocks of texts. Once they complete each word, it becomes a visual of the word that you can click on for synonyms (thereby simultaneously acquiring a larger repository of vocabulary). The fourth station is built on a game such as Tetris or even Angry Birds© where students use play, spatial understandings, and imagination to move through immersive, game environments to build on and reinforce problem-solving and spatial strategies in digital spaces. The final station focuses on returning to the originals, as well as new collective texts, by having a block of text on a topic and having every student add to the content to make it a collective text.

As with reading, writing in multimodal times has changed significantly. Composition is a more fitting way of describing the process of producing a text. The twenty-first-century literacy classroom demands a broadening of writing to include new compositional practices and processes, such as the notion of 'remixing'.

In their book about the new culture of learning, Douglas Thomas and John Seely Brown describe remixing as 'changing three big things' (Thomas & Seely Brown, 2011: 22). That is, taking one text and not only making it into something else, but also 'to get it as good as possible and if it needs improvements, you are happy to have others remix' (Thomas & Seely Brown, 2011: 22). Remix moves beyond copying or even plagiarizing because it compels composers as speakers to 'improve' content and infuse their agency into the production by making choices about how to remix. Ideally, there should be a built-in system that identifies any remixed content to show the line of composers who have been a part of the remix process.

- Consider the last text you have remixed or added to something else, for example, a photo you have added to your *Facebook*.

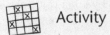 Activity

Remixing across Text Genres

To harness student understanding of multiple genres of texts and student knowledge base in relation to remixing one text into another text, put famous images or photographs around your classroom and create different

(Cont'd)

stations at each image. There should be no more than four students at each station with each member having a designated role (e.g., analyzer, researcher, producer/director and editor).

Ideally, each image pays homage to a historical event. For instance, profile such events as: the first person to walk on the moon; race riots; the first ultrasound of the womb, etc.

Then, ask each group to take the concept, elements of the visual and remix them into something else, whether it is a short film with a portable camera or a podcast about the historical event. The final stage of the assignment can be contributing to a class blog about remaking the visual into something else, thereby developing a meta-awareness of the remixing process.

These examples and accompanying activities illustrate how literacy and multimodality have moved on. This way of working allows teachers to harness tacit skills and practices so that our students acquire and transform them into assessable, even objective-driven skills that curricula demand.

- Think about an activity you could devise which does not rely on tablets but uses remix in similar ways. How would that work in your classroom? For example, a class notice board, blog, collage, art project, or exhibition all involve remix.

Theory Box: Karen Wohlwend on using toys for story inquiry

In her research and writing, Karen Wohlwend has explored the toys and artifacts that surround young children as consumers (Wohlwend, 2009). Through close analysis of commercial texts and products, Wohlwend examines the connection between commercialized products and children's meaning-making. Wohlwend uses a permeable curriculum incorporating Disney princess dolls and stories into writing workshop activities enabling children to replay and rewrite well-worn story lines and characters from Disney films to fuel their passions for literacy activities. Wohlwend recognizes that meaning-making for children is not governed by adult principles of genre of text, but is a much more fluid and complex process of remix.

DIGITAL LITERACIES

Recent research has looked at the way in which children draw on digitized culture to make meaning. Digitized culture includes the games and digital media that are prevalent in many homes today. Researchers such as Jackie Marsh look at children's popular culture and literacy to examine how **cultural resources** like PlayStation games can uphold children's narrative identity (Marsh, 2005). Research has highlighted how the curriculum can incorporate children's use of the Internet, email, SMS messaging, texting, PlayStation and other digital media. Gee, for example, argued that videogames have a part to play in literacy learning (Gee, 2003). Multiliteracies is also a development from the 1990s as a curriculum that acknowledges the many literacies that children experience and can shape, in a future curriculum (Cope & Kalantzis, 2000).

Clearly, a key shift in literacy education has been an acceptance of the notion of digital literacies. As far back as 1995, Richard Lanham maintained that 'digital literacy enables us to match the medium we use to the kind of information that we are presenting and to the audience we are presenting it to' (Lanham, 1995: 3). Lanham is saying that when we enter this domain of meaning-making, there is a logic to be engaged with that is also linked to commercial ideas of design. Maybe it is a logic that is less visible in classrooms but it helps to understand it.

- Think of how a commercial product has been designed, such as a mobile phone or a notebook. How can you apply those design principles in your classroom?

Michele Knobel and Colin Lankshear (2007) complement this perspective with a socio-cultural perspective based on the work of James Paul Gee, and in so doing, they help us to broaden our definition of a reified notion of digital literacy to digital **literacies**, taking account of becoming digitally literate as the mastering of multiple Discourses (Gee, 1996, 1999a). Knobel and Lankshear began a process by which researchers understood that the digital was everyday. The digital can be hand-made, local and crafted by practice. It is not an alien thing, such as a set of computers in a classroom (e.g., discourse around ICT), but embedded into bus journeys and everyday practices.

Talking about 'socially mediated ways of generating meaningful content through multiple modes of representation', Donna Alvermann (2008) adds to the conversation, pointing to explicit skills that arise from digital texts such as wikis, blogs and web pages that are the medium for social interaction. Alvermann highlights that digital readers and writers need to make many decisions online and, as such, they need to have a critical eye towards different genres of texts and a meta-awareness of these texts as promoting or silencing particular views (2008: 16). Julia Davies looks at different affinity groups, from Wiccan girls to transnational youth (Davies, 2006), on web pages to show how individuals find solace in online communities and how online communities foster identities and communities. Other researchers have spotlighted the role that new literacies play in online conversations (Chandler-Olcott & Mahar, 2003), videogaming (Steinkuehler & King, 2009 and Abrams, 2010), and writing fan fiction (Black, 2009).

- What digital communities do you belong to?

Digital literacies covers such wide and varied fields that look across text genres signalled earlier, such as:

- fanfiction;

- texting;

- podcasting;

- voicethreading;

- skyping.

In a commentary, Elizabeth Moje helpfully prompts researchers to pay attention to the range of practices different groups engage in (Moje et al., 2004). Obviously, we need to acknowledge, incorporate, and build on digital or new literacies in our classrooms. There is a range of practices that are tacit, even natural for many students. However, there are also some hidden tensions about digital literacies. Who has these technologies in our classroom is a pressing question. Whether we, as educators, have access to tablets and laptops is yet another pressing question. For now, we work with and improvise on what we have to hand and we are thoughtful about the dispositions that digital literacies imply.

 Activity

Making Texts from Multiple Resources

Make a list of the resources you have to hand around making a text in your classroom. Brainstorm these, if you can, with the students. Ask the students to create a text using whatever digital or material resources they choose. Ask them to plan the activity, and then to work in small groups around their chosen text type, such as a film, PowerPoint, scrapbook, visual exhibition or piece of writing. Display these and show other students or teachers what you have produced in a final dissemination event. What kinds of texts did students decide to use and why?

Theory Box: Mary P. Sheridan and Jennifer Rowsell on 'Fearless creativity' through **design literacies**

To access and extrapolate the perspectives of new media and digital technologies, producers Mary Sheridan and Jennifer Rowsell interviewed 30 producers to explore their logic and language for producing 'texts' (e.g., toys, videogames, movies, TV shows) for the marketplace. Their research identified a framework comprising four stages:

- Spinning an idea into a design;

- Designing the spin;

- Remixing and converging the idea into branded items;

- Using social networking to promote the text and give it life.

As a formula for text production, producers viewed these four stages as exhibiting what they call 'fearless creativity'. Learning in the twenty-first-century implies these skills and a disposition for trial and error until you find the right design and fitting modes to express the spin. Design, and its nuances and its logic, is central to a twenty-first-century literacy mindset (Sheridan & Rowsell, 2010).

ARTIFACTUAL LITERACIES

Multimodality should not be equated with computers, tablets and new communicational systems. Multimodality is age-old. To balance perspectives within multimodality and view it as nested within a longer history meaning-making and improvisation, we have researched the notion of 'artifactual literacies' (Pahl & Rowsell, 2010). In our work together, we use the terms 'artifact' and 'object' interchangeably, but we focus principally on the idea of the **artifact**. The notion of artifact can be defined as a thing or object that:

- has physical features that makes it distinct, such as colour or texture;

- is created, found, carried, put on display, hidden, evoked in language or worn;

- embodies people, stories, thoughts, communities, identities and experiences;

- is valued or made by a meaning maker in a particular context.

Artifacts bring in everyday life. They are material, and they represent culture. They can link literacy, multimodality and material culture together by focusing the lens on meaning-making that is situated and material. Artifacts open up stories and give opportunities for telling stories. Every object can tell a story: many objects carry many stories within them. These stories are repeated in interaction and remain continually told and re-told to visitors, changing in the process. Artifacts can connect worlds, as they travel between worlds. When a child connects to literacy and is asked to write a story, this is the end of a long process of meaning-making that could begin in a different setting, in the everyday. For example, a child could love toy cars and be obsessed with collecting them. This interest spills into a story about cars. In school, this could then be told or written as a narrative text and/or crafted as a digital story.

Artifactual literacy opens up a new world that celebrates different sorts of values: the hand-made (Whitty, Rose, Baisley, Comeau & Thompson, 2008), the sensory (Pink, 2009), the storied (Hurdley, 2006), and the material (Miller, 2008). In letting new kinds of disciplines into literacy, literacy looks different. We think it looks artifactual, and it offers a challenge for curriculum makers to listen to unheard voices. To conceptualize artifactual literacy requires an understanding of literacy as a situated social practice together with literacy as *materially* situated. This then brings in the everyday world of objects and stories to create meaning.

Children draw on their artifactual experiences as a resource for meaning-making. Artifacts are objects to grow with. Many students have a favourite stuffed toy they recall from early childhood, that they still treasure. Children also identify the stages of childhood through their objects. Here is Sam, age 8, talking about his objects:

> I've always been changing my subject. When I was a baby I liked wheels, then I liked Thomas the Tank Engine, then I liked Robots, I liked Space then I liked Pokémon through seven and a little bit of eight, then I'm into Warhammer now I've moved on from the rest of my – I was getting bigger all those eight life years. (Interview, Kate Pahl, November 20, 2001)

Artifacts lever power differently in classroom settings. For example, in a project called 'All About Me', which involved asking parents and children to work jointly to fill shoeboxes to represent the children's identities, and was conducted with 5–6-year olds in Bristol, the project team found out that the object boxes opened up new worlds in new ways:

> It was noticeable that some of their boxes contained some very personal items – a first babygro, a page from the local paper in which the child had featured in an article on a children's bereavement service, a book called

'You Are Special', presented to the child at nursery school. There were also items given or created by other people in the child's family. Karim's box, for example, contained lists of his hobbies and the names of family members, created by his older brothers and sisters. (Greenhough et al., 2005: 99)

The project enabled the children to bring their home identities into school, but also had a powerful role in inspiring writing. Some of the writing was strong and let in new emotional spaces (Scanlan, 2008). The children's writing referred to the special objects they had brought in. A mother of one of the children commented:

It's nice to show things from home. I think there's a certain bit of security there, these are familiar pieces that he's taken in and he enjoys and then suddenly they're in a different context, they're in a school context, and I think that's nice. ... And what was funny was sometimes it might not be the things in your own box that inspire you, it would be things in somebody else's box. (Greenhough et al., 2005: 100–101)

The experience of talking about an object can open up new worlds and domains of practice. A domain is a world where things happen. It is often tied to a specific place or space, such as a home, a community or a church (Barton & Hamilton, 1998). Artifacts are often found within households but travel across sites and domains to become meaningful. Found artifacts tie communities to their history. Bringing an artifact into school can change the discussions that take place. For example, children may have family artifacts that signal a family's history. Some artifacts can stand for a memory or a historical event. They may become held in a museum exhibition, taken to school or rearranged on a mantelpiece. Artifacts are entangled within identities and can be evoked and reanimated within narratives. Artifacts can open up new worlds of experience. Talking about artifacts provides ways into narratives that are not always accessible in other ways. They can be used to encourage children to respect diversity, to find points of commonality across communities, and can be used as important starting points for literacy learning. Artifacts are also key ingredients for family stories, that provide meaning and direction for lives lived in communities. Collective and social memories are helped and brought into new spaces through family stories and artifacts (Brooke, 2003).

- Think of and plan a lesson around artifacts in your classroom.

THINKING CRITICALLY ABOUT MULTIMODALITY

There is a pressing need for students to build on tacit skills they bring with them and an equal need for them to critically frame these same tacit skills, which they often do not bring with them. To interrogate multimodality, we offer teachers the following objectives:

- Establish the truthfulness and reliability of online texts.

- Think analytically about all texts that they use by asking questions.

- Identify hidden messages or preferred readings that pertain to bias, stereotypes, and maybe even hypocrisy.

- Examine language used and how language works across other modes.

- Locate social and cultural views in texts and ask 'Who has the power in this text?'

- Ask yourself 'What social norms are reinforced by this text?'

- Interrogate text designs. What is the dominant mode? What other modes are used? Why these modes and not others?

- Interpret how a text should be read and ask 'What are other alternative readings?'

These activities are not about the language, but about the images and design. It is easy to slide over content. A critical lens on design is often missing from classrooms. As educators, we need ways to unpack why texts look a certain way. Describing multimodal texts is a missing piece of critical literacy in relation to the multimodal work students need to do.

- How would you analyze a multimodal text in the classroom?

Vignette: Multimodal assemblages

By Kari-Lynn Winters

Kari-Lynn Winters' teacher candidates at Brock University are handing in their final assignments for their Drama in Education course. Unlike other university courses, these assignments are not essays or exams, but they are what Kari-Lynn calls 'multimodal assemblages' – these multimedia collections demonstrate the candidates' thinking processes and voice their understandings of the class content. These assignments often include:

- Personal responses to class activities;

- Examples of how to apply drama and literacy strategies learned in class;

- Theoretical frameworks that relate to the candidates' interests, beliefs, and areas of study;

- Data collected during and beyond class time;

- Research questions the teacher candidates would like to continue exploring;

- Cultural artifacts such as clothing, photography, music clips.

These assemblages demonstrate learning and personal inquiry through an array of text forms.

Each assemblage is distinct. While some teacher candidates primarily focus on visual texts, such as scrapbooking, painting, and drawing, others choose words to create narratives or poetry. Kinesthetic, musical, and digital texts have also been included in the forms of DVDs, *YouTube* videos, CDs, websites, blogs, and Prezi presentations. It is not uncommon to see maps, magazine collages, photographs, sketches, or video clips.

The teacher candidates draw on the affordances of various texts, demonstrating that they are both external and internal meaning makers who are capable of and often do orchestrate a multiplicity of modes in their daily lives. During this assignment these candidates become sophisticated and critical authors, as Kari-Lynn calls them, who continually shift among the social (inter)actions of design, negotiation, production, and dissemination as they interpret and communicate meaning to create storylines of their class work and relationships.

Multimodal assemblages consider authorship broadly. They posit that meaning-making is not an isolated or stable phenomenon, but is bound up with semiotic, social, and critical meanings that interrelate with and inter-animate one another.

CONCLUSION

On a practical level, within the classroom, children need to understand texts and how texts are put together to use and make them themselves. Texts and the meanings within texts are tied together. If texts are viewed as artifacts, which are made by certain people (e.g., child and adult), in certain social contexts, with certain functions in mind, they can be explored further. If texts are digital, they have different affordances. They might be made by larger corporations, but they can also be made, mediated or remixed by a local person. These local/global interactions need to be explored further. We would like to put artifactual literacies together with digital literacies to understand meaning-making further.

One activity to try with older students is to consider different newspapers. If you juxtapose three different newspapers, you will find that each one is speaking to a certain reader and reflects certain values. Differences among the three papers materialize in the tone and the style of the writing as much as they materialize in the layout, font and format. The articulation of content and design speaks to a particular person in a particular situation. Like an archaeological artifact, aspects of a text's materiality are clues to who made it, when, how and why.

When teaching, it helps to suggest to students that books are physical, live artifacts with a story and system lying behind them. By 'live' we mean that people working in a place through a set of practices brought its physical state into being. What does this have to do with teaching literacy? Viewing the texts children use and make in class in this light gives them a far deeper understanding of genre, design, editing, and language than restricting literacy to balancing phonics instruction with whole language. On the whole, children understand by doing and by using symbolic practices – whether with image, music, or written text – and understanding texts as artifacts of practices facilitates a more meaningful engagement with language.

Children's texts go to school

Vignette: Honouring home literacy

Stacey is a young mother of four young children. All her children were born prematurely and had health difficulties. Stacey was keen to share books with her children. A local family support organization gave Stacey a bag of toys, called 'Bags for Families', which consisted of a tent made of netting for imaginative play and a book. Stacey recorded, using a video camera, her own family reading practices:

- We have turned our stuff into a little reading corner. As you can see we have got the drape and the rug and they are reading nice books together! What is your book, Cameron? What is your book, Lucy? Your book's a train book, isn't it?

- Cameron says he is going to use it for his cars. He says he is going to use it for a garage.

Stacey used the imaginary play space, provided in the form of a drape and a rug, to make a reading corner for her young children.

Key themes in the chapter:

- Drawing on the everyday to make meaning
- Research on home/school literacy
- Re-thinking boundaries between home and school
- What counts as literacy learning at home?
- Bringing home to school
- What can we learn from families?

INTRODUCTION

Imagine that you are in a classroom – teaching or observing or working at your desk – and you see one of your students reading a comic book or drawing/making a picture of a bird instead of working on his maths or language activities. At first, you might think that he is avoiding doing work. However, digging deeper, you find that he does not understand the task at hand and reverts back to what he can do and what interests him.

- How would you react in this situation?

- Could it be a situation when you can build on what he knows and likes in the lesson at hand or another aspect of your lesson?

What can be observed is that this child is at the interface between group knowledge (i.e., what his fellow students are doing) and individual knowledge (i.e., what he carries with him). Literacy practices can be combined from home, and meanings that are carried with them, and then transformed in school into new knowledges and discourses.

This chapter focuses on homes and literacy. What do we imagine when we think about homes and literacy? Our experience of homes is often drawn from what we know. To understand literacy in the homes of the children in our classrooms requires going beyond this existing knowledge into others' lives. By recognizing different kinds of home literacy practices, it is possible to make sense of children's literacy practices in school settings. Home literacy practices can remain invisible to schools unless there is time to listen to them. Homes carry literacies of migration (Pahl & Pollard, 2010). Homes are material spaces, strewn with objects, linked to stories. They often include digital equipment that can be used to make meanings, often across generations. Artifacts contribute to the stories and texts children share in homes (Pahl & Rowsell, 2010).

- Think about your own home, as an adult or child, and describe it as a material world with artifacts and as carrying stories.

In this chapter, we also focus on the ways in which literacy can be used between family members. Families can teach us about literacy. We can begin to appreciate the ways in which families themselves hold a plethora of literacy practices within their homes. Recent research (Marsh, 2011) helps us to understand that literacy practices are embedded in popular cultural practices. Literacy can be found embedded in popular songs, within electronic equipment and software, within malls and signage (Marsh, 2005). These all are resources within homes. There is a diversity of cultural practices in homes. Story sharing can be done in so many ways in homes; in different languages, using animation on the computer, using games and puzzles as well as with actual books. Many print-based activities are inscribed in games and craft as well as material objects. The experience of growing up in a home is embodied and sensory (Mackey, 2010). This chapter will build on Chapter 2 in that the multimodal nature of home literacy practices will be fully discussed so that teachers can account for multimodal and digital literacies in their classrooms.

Since the first edition of *Literacy and Education*, we have focused more on material worlds in homes and what they signal about literacy practices and the notion of **sedimented identities in texts** (as profiled in Chapter 5). In this chapter, we introduce some research on home literacy. Research on home literacy has come from a number of disciplines, including psychology, anthropology and sociolinguistics. Reading research on material culture in homes has helped us to understand home literacy practices. For example, Daniel Miller, in *The Comfort of Things* (2008), describes the power of objects to shape lives and identities, and presents a strong picture of how objects carry people forward with them. We have found, in our work on *Artifactual Literacies* (Pahl & Rowsell, 2010), that artifacts can support literacy learning as they call up home experience in new ways. We need a research strategy that tracks the connections from home, to community contexts and then to school contexts to take account of home literacy.

- Map out where your home sits within the community and your key local hubs.

Much of this research is underpinned by a belief that children's literacy comes from home, and *the home is where children learn much of their literacy skills*. Most of the research also recognizes the importance of parents in supporting their children. McNaughton (2001) described how family activities form the prime socialization activities, with schools providing the secondary space. At the beginning of this chapter, Stacey takes her children into her little reading corner. This is fundamental to home literacies. Anning describes home literacies here:

> We observed that for some of the children their meaning making at home remained a consuming interest. They created a secret world of home-based personal narratives, often informed by popular culture and imagery or based on passions for fashion, football, pop music or video imagery. These

personal representations were strongly informed by gendered interests modelled within their communities of practice, often shared across several generations and modelled in extended family networks. (Anning, 2003: 32)

These representations can be found strewn across many homes. Increasingly, multimodal representations include online communicative practices such as blogs, *YouTube* videos, games and downloaded images from the internet (Wohlwend, 2010; Yamada-Rice, 2010).

- How are your multimodal practices at home both digital and non digital?

This chapter will combine a focus on current research, with examples of how home/school literacies can be considered in relation to classrooms. In order to look at home and school literacy, researchers have come up with an important way of distinguishing between the two. Rather than see the literacy children do at school as the only form of literacy, researchers have identified the literacy children do at school as **schooled literacy**, tied to the school domain. By contrast, **out-of-school literacy**, which can take place in many diverse sites, including homes, community centres and street corners, is sometimes very different. Teaching and learning take place in many spaces, and students will absorb information unexpectedly and in different places, for example, at home, in play schemes, clubs, or activity centres. When students are in the classroom, they will sometimes pay attention and sometimes not. Students' attention and interest will ebb and flow in and out of their experience of teaching. By bridging a gap between home and school, it is possible to allow them in far more.

LITERACY ACROSS HOME AND SCHOOL

It is important to conceptualize the relationship between home and school literacy practices. This enables us to recognize where children's literacy practices sit. Below, we have conceptualized this as a quadrant.

 Points of Reflection: Identifying literacy practices across home and school

If you look at the four quadrants opposite, which quadrant can you see your practice within? Where do you think literacy is situated?

Literacy is something you do at school It is best left to teachers to do literacy Literacy only involves print and is about academic and school success *1 = school literacy*	Literacy is something that you can practice at home This is in order to get ready for school, for example, using books and letters to help children at school but in the home *2 = school based literacy at home*
Literacy at home is a different thing, and involves a number of practices, including: Texting, computer games, graffiti, TV, and is embedded in toys and stories Popular culture literacies, visual, digital and multilingual literacies *3 = diverse home literacies but not at school*	Literacy is about merging home and school practices Diverse literacies at home can be used in school and merged with school literacy to create successful literacy learning. These practices can include both quadrant 2 and 3 to support quadrant 4? *4 = diverse home and school literacies*

Figure 3.1   Four models of literacy at home and at school

Part of the challenge for educators is to move from quadrant 1 to quadrant 4, and for those working with families to hear the literacy practices in quadrant 3.

The location of literacy practices is clearly important in this analysis. We have drawn on thinking from Barton and Hamilton's *Local Literacies* (1998) to help distinguish between the setting where literacy takes place and the worlds of literacy children inhabit.

〰️   Points of Reflection: How can we understand these two spaces?

Researchers have used words such as domain and site to look at home and school literacy (Barton & Hamilton, 1998). A domain is the sphere where a literacy practice originally was created and used. A site is the place where the literacy practice is actually engaged with. For example, homework is an activity where the domain is school, but the site is home. The chart below describes how homework can be seen in relation to domain and site.

Homework analyzed by site and domain

Domain	Site
School	Home

The flow of texts across from school to home and then back again is something that can then be analyzed. Where texts go, whether they stay at home or return back to school, is something to track. Learning at home can look different, as can literacy at school. Here we explore literacy as it materializes in home settings.

- Document literacy practices completed in one day.

WHAT DO WE COUNT AS LITERACY LEARNING AT HOME?

In this section, we consider what literacy can look like in homes. Literacy begins with the marking of the page, with a pen or pencil, as a form of inscription (Ingold, 2007). Children can inscribe meaningful marks on the page when they are very young. When children begin to write, they often draw and narrate their worlds in the form of drawing plus writing (Pahl, 1999). We recognize this as a form of multimodal meaning-making (Jewitt & Kress, 2003). Multimodality is a taken-for-granted part of communicative practices. When children compose in the classroom, their composing process is accompanied by play, gesture, drawing and talk. Students may use drama, songs, photography, multimedia, such as *Facebook*, blogs and wikis and digital storytelling as well as everyday practices such as texting, emailing and craft activities to communicate meaning. Increasingly, young children, as well as older children, access digital tools such as text messaging, *Facebook*, virtual worlds such as Club Penguin and Moshi Monsters, as well as interactive games and games consoles as part of their communicative practices. Children can move quite naturally across the surfaces of the screen, adding images, decorating text, and inscribing bits of words and language into their multimodal texts (Kress, 1997).

By widening the scope of what literacy is, and seeing it as embedded in different kinds of objects, such as craft materials and within digital texts, literacy is seen as one of a number of communicative practices children engage in. Literacy can be found embedded in many forms, such as textiles, craft materials, online presentations and assemblages such as scrapbooks, as seen in Kari-Lynn Winters' vignette in Chapter 2. In a study of home writing practices that I (Kate) carried out, children sewed their name on materials, made craft objects such as book marks and embroidery samplers, and created collages, with writing inscribed within these objects.

- Can you find something at home with inscribed writing?

In home and community contexts, many researchers have looked at how children engage in a number of communicative practices at the same time – perhaps listening to a CD while writing a diary, or text messaging with friends while doing homework. A child may be on one website to chat with friends, while doing homework on another screen. Or, a child may be playing a console game and find tips on a chat-line or website (a bit like cheat sheets) on how to move to the next section of their game. Therefore, when discussing children's out-of-school literacies, a wider range of communicative practices is drawn upon. We can call these **multimodal literacies** (Flewitt, 2008). These literacies are made up of different forms and meanings. Children's texts will be seen as **crossing** sites, moving into different domains, and changing as they do so.

DRAWING ON THE EVERYDAY TO MAKE MEANING

Understanding home literacy means understanding the everyday because **multimodal literacy** practices are often situated within the everyday. Gunther Kress described the ways in which children come to make meaning quite naturally, drawing on the 'stuff' they find. In *Before Writing*, he described this:

> Children see the complexity of the meaningful cultural world with absolute clarity; and in their making of meaning they construct, elaborate, complex, representations of that world – out of the materials which are to hand: bits of paper, glued, stuck, cut, folded, painted, cut out; bits of tinsel; old birthday cards, coloured string; and so on. (Kress, 1997: 33)

Gunther Kress observed the ephemeral 'messing about' that young children do in home settings, a kind of invisible and hastily tidied away meaning-making practice Kate observed in her own study (Pahl, 2002). This kind of home meaning-making is sometimes not visible. One way of honouring home meaning-making is to give young children scrapbooks that they can carry between sites, for example, between home, and school and community contexts.

Vignette: Drawing on the everyday to make meaning

As part of a study of literacy practices in a library, I (Kate) worked with a group of young people to explore how they use literacy in a library. This was part of a project called 'Research Rebels', a participatory research project with young people about the uses of literacy in homes and in a community setting, a library. Bonni and Dionne, both aged 12, made a scrapbook using books provided by the project, and then drawing

(Cont'd)

on material cut out and stored at home. Here, Bonni and Dionne talk about cutting out:

Dionne: In the library we started sticking our pictures in and we got bored at school so Bonni messed about with the Tippex in Spanish and started writing stuff and then she started sticking pictures in.

Kate: How did you choose the pictures?

Dionne: Well Bonni and me had a camera and we used some of the film at my house and some at her house and we had like six left and so we used them when we went to Much Wenlock on holiday.

Here, however, Dionne sees this practice retrospectively; it was what Bonni used to do 'when we were bored at school'. The two young people jointly reconstructed their past selves in the scrapbooks. For example, Bonni included a picture of herself as a young child to signal this 'self' that used to be:

Figure 3.2   Bonni as a child

In the vignette, the girls talk about their past selves, and the way in which the meaning-making drew on their collage practices at home. This page opposite was assembled using Tippex, cut-out images, small cut-out dictionary definitions and a photograph of Bonni. All of these were to hand in their home.

Kress' concept of what is 'to hand' can also be described as being 'stuff', that is, material ephemera that is not easily classifiable. The concept of 'stuff' from Miller (2010) helps us to understand the ways in which children's texts are assemblages of what is 'to hand' and this understanding informs how we can view children's text-making in home settings. In the following vignette, also from Bonni and Dionne, they describe the stuff they had to hand in their homes, which included classroom notes.

Vignette: Taking account of 'stuff'

Bonni and Dionne described the layers of 'stuff' that they drew on to make their scrapbooks:

Kate: Where did you get the ideas to put the different things in like colour?

Dionne: Bonni had this blue folder and it was full of cut up pictures and Bonni just went through it and put them in piles.

Bonni and Dionne used their scrapbooks to recall their past writing identities. They were fascinated by their childhood writing selves:

Kate: This is a good page as well.

Dionne: That's one of Bonni.

Kate: Is that one of your drawings when you were little?

Girls: Yeah.

Dionne: She did a little note saying to mum: 'this is just a little note to tell you how much I love you'. (That's embarrassing by the way).

Kate: I love it.

Dionne: She used to write backwards!

(Cont'd)

Figure 3.3 Bonni's special note

The way in which children compose texts is constructed both by the timescales of the past and of the present, and of the future (Compton-Lilly, 2010). When we consider children's meaning-making at home, the identities of children do not reside so much in their year group, but within their past and future selves. Above, Bonni and Dionne talk about their past writing practices. When thinking about home literacy practices, *timescales*, the way texts are linked to different generations and different stories in the home, as well as the *spaces and places* children inhabit, are all-important. For example, a text may be tied to a grandparent's story, or an object collected by a grandparent in the past (Pahl, 2004). Texts are also linked to objects. In our book, *Artifactual Literacies* (Pahl & Rowsell, 2010), we explored how objects called up different spaces, often those that were not visible within the classroom, such as countries children had migrated from, or where their grandparents still lived. The spaces that children's texts link to are worth considering when we make sense of them in the classroom. *Therefore, the image of children's texts crossing sites is important in this chapter.*

Theory Box: Anne Haas Dyson on recontextualizing texts

A piece of theory which helps us understand what happens when children's text-making goes to school is **recontextualization**. This word has been used to describe the movement of children's texts across sites from one domain to another. Anne Haas Dyson uses this word to describe how children take texts or practices from one domain, and move them across sites, mixing them up as they do so (Dyson, 2003). When children's texts cross boundaries, they can be recontextualized into the new setting. The idea of recontextualization, that is, moving a piece of writing or drawing which was done in one context to another context, and embedding it in a different discursive space, is important when considering how children's texts cross sites. These issues can be applied to any setting: school, college or community centre.

Returning to the scrapbooks, the writers, Bonni and Dionne, call up identities that are past (the writing they did as children) as well as present selves. The scrapbooks represent a boundary between their past and their present selves, as well as moving between home and school.

- Find a boundary object at home and bring it to school to show your students. Ask students to think and write about boundary (past and present) objects.

The mixing that happens in the scrapbooks is a textual practice that needs to be recognized, as children mix and remix texts across the domains of home and school and community (Dyson, 2003). This remix requires an understanding of the literacy curriculum as permeable, that is, it lets in different kinds of voices and textual practices.

Bringing down boundaries between home and school requires interaction. Educators have drawn on strategies such as *culturally responsive literacy teaching* (Gay, 2000). This means drawing on home cultures to make sense of texts in the classroom. It might involve using different modes, for example, oral or visual modes to open up discussion. Working with children or young people on their home literacy practices might involve a different kind of conversation. When we work with students on their meaning-making, we need to take account of the different quality of talk that this creates. For example, when we ask a student about their home artifacts, this opens up a new space, which lets in home experience. In school settings, this can create a different kind of talk, and narratives can become fuller and more detailed (Pahl & Rowsell, 2010). In our work using objects to support literacy, we have found that listening to young people describe their objects can open up new spaces.

Vignette: Talk about artifacts

In a project involving a group of high school students bringing objects into class and talking about them, Jennifer interviewed Alicia about her valued objects. The combination of interview talk and interviewee engagement with artifacts offered a window into what a participant valued and why they valued particular material qualities of artifacts. For example, when Jennifer asked about what she likes about her gold bracelet, Alicia said the following:

Jennifer: So ... Alicia, tell me about your bracelet.

Alicia: Well, um, this bracelet came from my great grandmother who gave it to my grandmother who gave it to my Mom, who gave it to me.

Jennifer: Do you wear it all the time?

Alicia: I wear it all the time because it makes me feel like I am carrying my family around, well like, I know they are always there for me.

Figure 3.4   Alicia's intergenerational artifact

As Alicia talked about the handing-down of her bracelet from one generation to the next, she touched the embossed flowers and pointed to small dents in them and how worn the bracelet had become with time. There was such a contrast between the timid Alicia I observed during class time and her animation as she talked about the intergenerational bracelet that she wears every day.

In this vignette, the power of talk as connective and as a way of creating a relational pedagogy that respects home learning through objects is evoked. Bringing home objects into school creates different kinds of relationships and evokes the narratives and cultural experience of students.

 Activity

Artifacts of Identity

Find an object at home that signifies you. The artifact can reflect elements of your background or it hints at deeper values and convictions or it can even reflect your teaching mantra. Once you have modelled your own artifact, then ask students to bring an artifact from home that similarly embodies or represents them. For the lesson, ask students to get into pairs and share their artifacts. Then, students can work independently on narratives about a moment involving the artifact. Like Alicia's bracelet above, a thing, an object opens up worlds and narratives.

THE STUFF OF EVERYDAY LITERACY

One aspect of home literacy that is interesting is what it looks like. It can look less like literacy and more messy, ephemeral and invisible (Pahl, 2002). Children can easily take photographs, using disposable cameras, of their home literacy practices. In a study Kate conducted with Margaret Lewis and Louise Ritchie, exploring families' literacy practices at home, funded by Booktrust, children took pictures of their home literacy practices (Pahl, Lewis & Ritchie, 2010). Books were found under beds, in bunk beds, on windowsills, and linked to a number of different practices in homes. Writing was also found in playhouses, on book marks, on embroidery, craft and collage activities. The materiality of literacy was clear when analyzing these photographs. In the vignette below, two girls from a British Asian heritage, whose family was originally from Pakistan, introduce me to their home literacy practices.

Vignette: Craft as literacy practices

When I arrived, the girls, Lucy (pseudonym) and Tanya (pseudonym), were wearing matching orange shalwar kameez. The family are Muslims, with a heritage from Pakistan. The girls were born in the UK. They live in a terraced

(Cont'd)

street, which has an old-fashioned feel with a sweet shop on the corner. For about a year and a half, I have been visiting to find out about the family's literacy practices. I had asked the girls to take pictures with a disposable camera and they produced these. I then produced two more. I was looking at a large A4 size painting of the letters of Tanya's name.

Kate: Can you tell me a bit about this please?

Tanya: I did it in my big sister's bedroom called Lucy. I used watercolours and I wrote it in my name and I have done lots of stories. And I used some glitter and I wrote some crystals.

Here, the name, written by an 8-year-old using glitter and crystals, is a literacy practice that is unregulated by school. In many examples of their writing, they focused on pocket books and purses embroidered with their names. In addition, the girls took photographs of their story books and of their everyday craft practices.

Figure 3.5 Literacy practices in the home

By doing ethnographic research on home literacy practices, I (Kate) was able to uncover the way in which these practices were linked to other activities, such as craft. By seeing the links between the craft activities and the inscribed writing, I could also understand meanings in the home more clearly. The stuff of everyday literacy therefore looks different from the stuff of literacy at school. How can these worlds be bridged?

BRINGING LITERACY FROM HOME TO SCHOOL

In this section, we consider how these home literacy practices can move into school. Children's home literacy practices are multimodal, and draw on different sites and domains for their inspiration. They are hybrid and diverse. One key source of influence is children's popular culture. Console games and other television narratives can be drawn upon to create new 'mixed' meanings. Children's texts describe different cultural worlds. Kenner's work (2000) details the different worlds a child inhabits. These worlds may include community contexts, such as mosque school, home contexts, such as particular traditions within the home, cultural influences from satellite television, and neighbourhood influences.

Here is an example, from Marsh (2003):

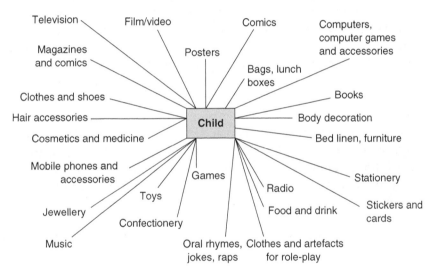

Figure 3.6 Children's popular cultural worlds
(Marsh, 2003: 114)

Anne Haas Dyson has watched children's literacy practices, and their artful mixing and composing, drawing on radio songs, playground rhymes and rich experiences across home and school to create a thread of meaning-making from all these sources. She describes this process as 'remix' to acknowledge how all these forms can provide inspiration for writing and composing processes (Dyson, 2003).

• Create a lesson based on the notion of remix and recontextualization.

What signals a difference between the first and second editions is the more prominent practice of remix as an everyday practice. Likewise, in her work on digitized literacies, Marsh has called for a revaluing of the textual meanings provided by children's popular culture, arguing that they offer a rich seam of meanings from which children can draw, write and orally re-tell stories (Marsh, 2003). Console games can become sources of narrative, often drawing on a number of different 'levels' in which to make new forms of meaning, layered and dependent on an understanding of how the games work (Pahl, 2005). Writing practices drawing on the digital world widen the scope of children's writing (Graham, 2009). These types of practice require a 'permeable' curriculum, in which children selectively combine influences from home and from school in their meaning-making, to make their meanings heard (Dyson, 2003).

Artifacts from popular culture are powerful spurs to meaning-making. In her work examining girls' interaction with dolls, Carrington (2003) explored how girls placed stories and narratives connected with dolls into a 'textual landscape' that merged popular culture with hybrid, multimodal literacy practices. Wohlwend (2009) showed how this kind of play with dolls extended literacy practices in classroom settings. She described how these toys are infused with anticipated identities that provide young children with rich seams from which to make meaning. The practice of authoring, as directors and composers, drawing on these multimodal and artifactual texts placed the young writers in an authorial space that was broader than the more static authoring generally provided for them in classroom spaces (Wohlwend, 2009: 76). The range of meaning-making drawing on home/popular culture ensembles is thus widened.

- How can schools draw on these practices and make sense of them in the classroom?

Many homes contain different cultural resources from that of schools. For example, many schools may not draw on children's popular culture, and do not see this as a resource when teaching children to write; at home, the word 'Barbie' may be a frequently written word. At school, images are less salient. At home, children may watch television, draw and play-act with more freedom. Parents may bring in their stories and their worlds to children's text-making. There is more latitude for subjectivities and identities in a home space compared to a school space.

This discussion links with a way of conceptualizing home literacy practices which recognizes what homes bring to literacy. This approach acknowledges how every home brings with it identities, dispositions, stories, objects, artifacts, memories, languages and resources. This implies a **wealth model** of literacy by which families' **cultural capital** can be drawn upon when planning schooled literacy activities.

Theory Box: Luis Moll on funds of knowledge

The wealth model has been linked to a number of theories and approaches. One is from Moll, who worked with Mexican-American parents (Moll et al., 1992; Gonzalez et al., 2005). He used the term 'funds of knowledge' to describe the cultural heritage and concepts parents bring to their children's literacies. Moll's work has influenced many educational researchers who have considered what homes bring to children's literacy practices. The wealth model often draws on detailed ethnographic work in homes to identify the resources families bring to literacy. In their joint book (Gonzalez et al., 2005), Moll's team describe how it is possible to research out-of-school literacy practices and funds of knowledge by conducting small-scale ethnographic studies. Carol Lee (2008) and Kris Gutiérrez and Barbara Rogoff (2003) argue for a more socially and culturally responsive pedagogy that takes account of these funds of knowledge. Elizabeth Moje and colleagues have drawn on this theory to make sense of young people's out-of-school experiences in the classroom, and argue for the creation of 'third spaces' in which young people's funds of knowledge from home can be valued, together with school literacy practices (Moje et al., 2004).

This linking between home and school has been noted as a key theme for researchers. Both Hull and Schultz (2002) and Street and Street (1991) have commented on how it is important to look at the continuities between home and school, rather than the discontinuities.

As a research area, the study of texts across sites has implications for how the home/school boundary is bridged. By tracking text-making across sites, home and school become places where rather than different activities being possible, the same activity is possible. In a study of a girl's plan from home, I (Kate) was able to observe how the influences for the text crossed from school to home and then back again (Pahl, 2007). The child, May, watched how map-making was carried out at school using squared paper. When she went home, her mother was drawing a plan of her new kitchen. Following her mother, she drew a plan of her house, describing what was important to her in the house. She then took this back to school to show to her teacher as an example of map-making. This was an example of home funds of knowledge being carried over to school.

In the following vignette we can see this process come to life in the form of a digital story.

Vignette: Artifactual literacies across home and school

In a research project called 'My Family My Story' carried out with a museum, a school and a small group of families with children aged about 8 or 9 and their siblings, we created stories about their favourite objects. These were first created as stories in a shoebox. Using disposable cameras, families brought back images of their favourite objects. They then wrote a story to go with the image, and told them again, together with images of the objects, to create digital stories. Digital stories are ensembles of meaning, made up of sound, moving image media, still photography, writing and drawing. They can be described as 'co-curated' by families as well as by practitioners (Potter, 2010).

Each session the families brought a further layer to their stories. When Lucy came back with her photographs taken at home, she was more specific. Here she is talking about the images she took: 'I took pictures of my two birds, of my candles. I have got a quartz stone. I took a picture of the bear. Jenni took a picture of the candle' (Digital audio tape, December 8, 2008).

Figure 3.7   Lucy's crystal

Lucy's daughter, Jennifer (9-years-old) interviewed her about the crystal:

Jennifer: What kind of photos did you take on the camera that hasn't been developed yet?

Lucy: I took my candles and I took my two bears and I took my quartz stone which is a pink stone.

Jennifer: Is it kind of like a crystal?

Lucy: Yes.

Jennifer: Anything else?

Lucy: My children. I think I took my children.

As Lucy became more engaged in the project, she began to reveal more of her life. In the final session, this interview was recorded and filmed by her daughter, Jennifer:

Lucy: I got this crystal off my friend because I have had a hard time in the last couple of years and she thought it would help and because I had that one I collect a few little ones as well.

Jennifer: Does it help?

Lucy: No (long pause, laughter) ... it looks nice! (long pause)

Jennifer: Does it feel special to you?

Lucy: Yes, because my very close friend gave me it.

In this vignette, Lucy slowly begins to develop a language around her favourite objects that she can share with her children, in ways that help both her and her daughter appreciate her feelings. In school, feelings, often linked to objects, sometimes seem quite powerful. However, objects are good conduits for emotion (Pahl & Rowsell, 2010).

How can objects connect up home experience with school? Pam Greenhough's work on objects going to school in shoeboxes (Greenhough et al., 2005) showed how the children were able to draw on their objects placed in shoeboxes, in a project called 'All About Me', and write more expressively about these objects in school. What struck the teacher/ researchers was how the children brought in forms of literacy from home that were not recognized as such at school:

> It is worth noting here that many of the boxes contained written or printed texts as items and many of these provide evidence of the 'textually mediated' texture of life outside school (Barton, 2001) of which the children are

a part. See, for example, the postcard from Disneyland, the birthday cards, the swimming certificate, the car park ticket, the newspaper report, the read-along video. (Greenhough et al., 2005: 99)

These 'other' forms of literacy can be linked and merged with 'school' literacy to create new, hybrid forms, in a 'third space' (Pahl with Kelly, 2005; Moje et al., 2004). This **third space** can include both forms.

Theory Box: Third space theory

One way to think about home and school is to consider a 'third space' where children can write out their home experiences. This can be, for example, a space where children can choose what they write about, or bring in artifacts from home to write about. The third space has been used to describe the in-between literacy practices of prisoners, who write to the outside world drawing on an 'in-between' space, neither the prison nor the outside world (Wilson, 2000). Wilson talked of the in-between literacies of prisons as offering prisoners a space in which to compose. Gutiérrez and colleagues use third space theory to consider ways in which culturally responsive pedagogical spaces can be forged from a blend of home languages and literacies in school spaces (Gutiérrez et al., 1999). If this theoretical space is given to children's meaning-making, what would it look like? By giving space to children's out-of-school literacies, many elements can come in. Third space can look like this:

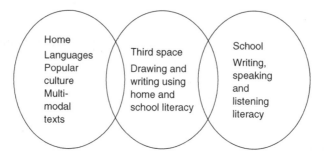

Figure 3.8   Third space

Third space theory allows us to think about how children's meaning-making often lies between school and home. Children compose and write in after-school clubs, or with friends, and when they compose at home they are drawing on school stuff and when they compose at school they are using their home experience and practices. Third space theory provides us with an understanding of literacy that is linked to spaces and provides a more *embodied* understanding of literacy.

- Identify a third space for you. Now use the concept in a lesson to reduce a gap between school and home spaces, for example.

Many texts produced by children have this quality of holding different cultural identities in one space. Millard (2003) described how one boy introduced into an adventure story pictorial narrative, the character of a devil man, who had 'come from one Sikh boy's memories of shared stories told to him by his mother' (Millard, 2003: 6). Children commonly mix culturally infused stories into their own richly blended narratives.

Part of the challenge for teachers is to create opportunities for children and young people to draw successfully on home experiences in classroom settings. Many educators try to bridge the gap between home and school, to meet parents on their own territory and listen to their experiences and resources. In this chapter, we build on that model and provide an account of home literacy practices which values what parents bring to literacy. The next section will begin by considering research on children's schooled literacy practices, and how they can be supported at home.

BRINGING LITERACY FROM SCHOOL TO HOME

In this section, we focus on literacy practices that start at school but then might go home. When a child arrives at school, the child begins school with a wealth of knowledge about the world to support his or her learning. Within school, this knowledge is translated into a focus on learning, and particularly a focus on literacy. Schooled literacy concentrates on lettered, alphabetic literacy, and its acquisition. Drawing on models of literacy development from psychologists such as Lev Vygotsky (1978), and researchers in the field of emergent literacy such as Marie Clay (1975), teachers work with children to foster their reading and writing skills.

Schools focus on books as being at the heart of this process. The reading of books became the centre of the strategies parents could be given by schools to support their children's literacy. The *book bag* is one example of this practice, whereby a child is sent home with a book to read. This is accompanied by a reading record, in order for the parent to communicate back to the teacher how the reading had gone.

Other ideas include *Storysacks*, which are bags with a book, and play items and artifacts connected to the story which children can do at home. Recent initiatives in bridging home and school have extended the storysacks idea to include *backpacks*. Inside the backpack are paper, pens, colouring pencils and writing equipment so that children can write stories at home and send them to school.

Book gifting schemes, such as the *Bookstart* pack initiative in the UK, which have provided free books to children at age 6 months, 18 months and 3 years, have been found to have had an effect on future engagement with books, with a particular effect showing up in the number of library books borrowed by parents after the end of the scheme (Bailey et al., 2002). Kate recently researched the effect of the *Imagination Library* scheme, which provides a free book a month to a child's home up until the age of 5 (Pahl et al., 2011). We have found in our research with families in Sheffield and Rotherham that families treasure books that are gifted in this way, and many connect the stories with other aspects of family life.

One of the very first studies on home/school literacy support by parents was by Tizard and Hughes, who looked in more detail at home/school support (Tizard & Hughes, 1984). They found that parents who supported their children's reading at home did better at school. This study led to many developments in schools, including the use of book bags, and links between home and school being strengthened.

Another key initiative which supports children's schooled learning and parents' own literacy skills is **family literacy** (Anderson et al., 2010). This initiative takes many forms, the chief one consisting of activities that involve literacy with both children and their parents. Dunsmore and Fisher (2010) recognize that family literacy is a concept that encompasses how families use literacy, and this might include everyday activities as described above. However, family literacy activities may also be initiated by the school and might include school-initiated literacy activities (Dunsmore & Fisher, 2010). Many schools encourage family literacy classes on site, and family literacy programmes are popular as offering a fun, supportive environment for children and parents to learn together. In the UK, an evaluation for the Basic Skills Agency's Family Literacy Programme, *Family Literacy Works* (Brooks et al., 1996) concluded that family literacy programmes offered parents and children a strong foundation for literacy.

• How can literacy practices in homes be fully recognized within communities and within family literacy classes?

In their study of mother/child shared reading at home, Je Eun Kim and Jim Anderson describe how the digital also shapes children's book-sharing experiences (Kim & Anderson, 2008). They describe how sharing electronic books in a very small-scale study in Canada led to more interactive talk between parents and children. The importance of books as interactive tools is useful for researchers of home literacy practices.

In a recent study in Sheffield (Pahl et al., 2010), of eight diverse families who made 196 films of home book-sharing practices, we looked at ways in which families shared books at home. In the study, we interviewed parents of children who had just received the books, and followed up their experience of book sharing by asking parents to make videos for us of how they shared the books with their children. We found that some parents could be described as *connective* book sharers, that is, they linked books to many other multisensory experiences and also to different times and spaces. For example, a father linked the story of 'Owl Babies' to an owl that lived in their garden. Connective book sharers shared books in many different times and spaces, including all through the day, out and about, on buses, and in different contexts. Books were not just for bedtime, and performed many different functions. They could be used to calm a child down, to provide sensory engagement, to make bath-time fun and to light up a dull moment.

- Ask your students to share different instances when they have read books at home.

Some parents focused more on the *skills* that books could provide, including print literacy and number counting. These parents would focus on practice and repetition in a range of skills, including kicking a ball, learning musical notes, and included in this repertoire was print literacy. There was evidence that this group focused on the drawing skills required to make the alphabet, and also the ability to read a book to oneself, rather than book sharing. This group had important things to teach us about the importance of practice, of repetition and of craft-based skills as life skills.

A more important sub-set of parents became increasingly focused on books as conduits for pleasure, emotion and sensory warmth between children and parents. The findings of this study indicate that by seeing books as for sharing, for pleasure and for emotional comfort, rather than, as schools tend to do, as a step on the way to reading, children responded positively. Parents who had not come across the idea of picture books as leisure were particularly likely to be in this group. For example, the family in the following Vignette, originally from Malaysia, were new to the idea of book sharing as a leisure activity.

Vignette: Colour Me Happy!

This episode was filmed by a mother, in a home. It shows a 5-year-old, Kai, sharing books with his father after school. The father, Abdul, is sharing 'Colour Me Happy' with Kai. This is Kai's favourite book from the Bookstart pack, called the 'Treasure Chest' – he will read no other stories. This episode, which lasted about one minute, was preceded by some bouncing around on the sofa by Kai. He is keen to share this book, and the atmosphere was warm and loving.

Kai:	I'd like this! (Kai and father are sitting closely together on sofa. There is a sense of anticipation)
Father:	What is this? (Kai gets book out of the Bookstart Treasure Chest)
Kai:	Colour me ... (Father traces words for son with his finger)
Kai:	(takes big breath) – H ... (Father laughs out loud)
Father:	Happy!
Kai:	Happy!
Kai:	(reading) Colour Me Happy! (Both father and son laugh together)

Here, a family began sharing books more frequently, just for pleasure. In a follow-up interview, they describe the impact of the pack:

Researcher (Kate):	One of the things that interested me, when you got the Bookstart pack and Treasure Chest, was what was your view?
Fay (mother):	It's leisure actually.
Kate:	Leisure?
Fay:	Reading as leisure and then you enjoy reading. I am not enforcing him to – you need to read and know what it is, just reading and – enjoy! Rather than, if I give this book he will start like (exaggerated), 'uuuh'. Storybook is for fun.

(From the Bookstart study, interview, February 19, 2010)

Here a family acknowledges the power of reading for fun in their home. This move is one that many families make, but in their own ways and on their own terms. Practitioners can learn from these many ways of book sharing, that can include loud, dramatic storytelling, soft, gentle storytelling, storytelling with gesture, sound, in different languages, in different modes and electronically as well as orally, with or without books. We found there were so many ways to share a book in the home.

HOME AND SCHOOL LITERACY BROUGHT TOGETHER

In this section we consider how to bring home and school together for literacy learning. It is acknowledged by schools now that families are the first support of children's literacy (Evangelou et al., 2009).

Theory Box: Peter Hannon and Cathy Nutbrown on the ORIM framework

A way of conceptualizing how parents could support children's literacy was the ORIM framework, developed by Peter Hannon, Cathy Nutbrown and Jo Weinberger at the University of Sheffield (Nutbrown et al., 2005). This gave parents a framework to use with their children that could be translated into literacy support for children's schooled literacy. Parents could provide:

- Opportunities for their children's literacy development (trips, visits, shopping, materials for writing, drawing, books, opportunities for play);

- Recognition of their literacy practices (explicitly valuing what children do, and listening to them talking playing and writing);

- Interaction with children to develop their literacy (such as spelling out words children want to write, looking at letter/sound names, helping children spell a word);

- Model their own literacy practices (reading signs, directions, instructions, packaging, print in the environment, writing notes, letters, shopping lists, reading newspapers).

(Hannon & Nutbrown, 1997)

The project was welcomed by families and had an impact on children's literacy development at school over time (Nutbrown et al., 2005).

Five years on, the ORIM framework continues to work well as a way of bridging home and school. When seen as a way of crediting home literacy practices, the ORIM framework has a powerful impact on the home/school literacy crossing. Evaluation of the use of the ORIM framework has also been very positive, particularly among teachers, who used it to discover how much parents were supporting their children's literacy at home (Hannon & Nutbrown, 1997). The Raising Early Achievement in Literacy (REAL) project collaborated with school teachers in developing a home-focused programme, based on the ORIM framework that was tried with over 80 families with pre-school children. The programme included home visits by the teachers. The project was welcomed by families and had an impact on children's literacy development at school over time (Nutbrown et al., 2005).

Many of these different ways of supporting children's literacy rest on studies which showed what children were doing at home before they came to school. A significant study was Wells' *The Meaning Makers* (1986), which followed children from a wide range of socio-economic backgrounds and their speaking, reading and writing at home and at school. Wells provided a key part of the home/school puzzle when the findings emerged that children from low socio-economic backgrounds engaged in a rich plethora of literacy practices at home.

As seen in Heath's (1983) study of children's literacy and language practices in three different communities, the arguments began to build up about the importance of recognizing children's specific literacy and language practices at home. Heath's study showed that in some homes the interaction between parents and children had certain qualities, which may not be the same as 'schooled' ways of interacting. Michaels' (1986) study of 1st Graders' oral interactions at school also found that particular children, in the case of her research African-American children, had ways of speaking which were not fully recognized in the 'schooled' domain.

Researchers studied oral communication in different cultures focusing on a number of different communities. They found that different communities, following Heath's insight, spoke and communicated differently. For example, Hymes (1996) looked at oral narrative skills in America's different communities. He argued that educators needed to listen to the patterns of storytelling different communities brought to the study of narrative (Hymes, 1996). Rodriguez-Brown (2010) argues that educators need to similarly account for the culturally-specific ways in which Latino families support their children's education. Programmes that recognize the 'linguistic practices, cultural practices, and knowledge that families bring to the learning situation' are more likely, therefore, to be successful (Rodriguez-Brown, 2010: 212).

Theory Box: Rebecca Rogers on literacy practices at home and at school

An ethnographic study by Rebecca Rogers (2003) also showed how one African-American family had strong and diverse literacy practices which were not duplicated in the schooled domain, but were unrecognized by school educators. In her study of the Treaders, an African-American family, many literacy practices were observed at home, but the daughter was considered Special Education material, and despite her struggles to remain in mainstream education, was not seen as mainstream. In Rogers' account, this was linked to a mis-match between home and school literacy practices, with home literacy practices not being valued by the school.

In the field of **multilingual literacies**, there have been a number of illuminating studies looking at how children's literacy develops at home, and then is supported at school. In Charmian Kenner's *Home Pages* (2000), she described how Billy, aged 3 years, 5 months, was immersed in a *literacy world* which included his country of origin, Thailand, his local community, including the Thai temple he attended, his school, where his mother helped out, his home, and his own interests and activities at home, including cartoons and videos he liked to watch (Kenner, 2000). By mapping Billy's literacy world, Kenner could see where and how literacy activities blended with school literacy activities, and where they were separate.

- Think of five students in your class to speak with about home literacy practices. Then find out what home literacy practices they engage in and how you can incorporate their home literacy practices into your schooling literacy practices.

Theory Box: Eve Gregory and Ann Williams on siblings and home/school literacy practices

In a study by Eve Gregory and Ann Williams of children growing up in the East End of London, siblings were important in developing children's schooled literacy practices. Through the familiar activity of 'playing school', younger siblings learned the rhythms and sounds of school literacy activities. Gregory and Williams used the term **syncretic literacy** to describe

(Cont'd)

how children took ways of doing literacy from school, and blended them with ways of doing literacy at home, or in the mosque school many children attended. They observed how children in community classes (mosque school) often had to repeat after the teacher, whereas this pattern is reversed in the English classroom. At home, children merged and blended these different patterns of interaction when they played school. They also looked at how intergenerational literacies were blended and merged with school literacy practices at home (Gregory & Williams, 2000; Gregory, 2001; Gregory et al., 2004).

Recognizing multilingual literacy practices in homes requires a different way of thinking about home/school links and connections. Below, we describe a study that considered how schools can link more closely with multilingual parents.

Theory Box: Adrian Blackledge on recognizing what multilingual parents can offer schools

In a study of Bangladeshi women in Birmingham, UK, by Adrian Blackledge (2000), the particular literacy practices of the mothers were not valued at school, and were not drawn upon in classroom activities. Blackledge made the following key suggestions for educators who wish to connect school and home when working with children and parents who speak other languages than English.

Schools can:

- make concerted efforts to communicate with families in their home languages;

- make explicit their understanding that community literacies, including oral literacies, contribute to children's learning;

- affirm families' cultural identity within and beyond the curriculum;

- make genuine attempts to involve parents in their children's education, including at a policy-making level (Blackledge, 2000: 69).

Blackledge is clear that there is an imbalance of power between home and school, particularly when women from different cultural identities do not have their own language recognized in the mainstream school system. These parents valued their spoken Sylheti language and their community language of Bengali, but did not see those languages recognized in the school their children attended. This disjuncture rendered the women powerless in their concern to support their children's learning (Blackledge, 2000: 68). This study shows how the coming together of home and school is sometimes difficult in the face of a misunderstanding of linguistic identities.

Blackledge and Creese (2010) have identified that children move quite naturally between languages, a process they describe as *translanguaging*. This process also can involve the use of popular cultural references, in both languages, and a movement across languages that is also multi-modal, producing an ensemble of multimodal, multilingual communicative practices. This kind of meaning-making, moving across languages, across modes, and deploying different cultural references from home and community contexts, is the norm in school and community contexts, argue Genishi and Dyson (2009). They argue that by seeing children's text-making as naturally multimodal and multilingual, the potentialities for meaning-making come alive.

Vignette: Telling a story in two languages

In a study of home book-sharing practices, one child, Mariam, whose first language was Arabic, traced over the pictures of a dual-language story book while narrating the story to herself. In the transcript of the video she can be heard saying 'I am Sarah' and telling the story of Goldilocks from her own perspective, tracing her finger over the image of the girl in the story, using Arabic and English interchangeably:

Mariam:	Sarah! (her name for Goldilocks) This Sarah. (She sucks the lollipop and follows the child in the storybook with her fingers.)
Mariam:	Has to take this. (She moves her arm along the book from the right to the left following the trees.)
Mariam:	There she is. (Points to figure on left.)
Zahra (mother):	Asks her daughter a question in Arabic (Mariam sits up and looks at her mother.)
Mariam:	There! (Her finger points to the Goldilocks figure.)

(Cont'd)

Figure 3.9   Mariam tracing the story with her finger
(From the Booktrust study, Pahl et al., 2010)

In this vignette, the child creates a dual-language text for herself, orally, assembling from two languages, Arabic and English, her own story of herself as Goldilocks. She switches quite naturally between languages. Blackledge and Creese (2010) talk about 'translanguaging' as a way of describing the switching between languages that children quite naturally do when they are speaking, drawing on a repertoire of different linguistic resources at any one time. Many practitioners who watch videos of home literacy practices acknowledge how much we have to learn from homes when considering supporting families with literacy.

WHAT CAN WE LEARN FROM FAMILIES?

Here we sum up the evidence of what we can learn from families. A study by Denny Taylor (1983) documented the rich vein of literacy practices in homes. Taylor's detailed ethnographic studies of American families suggested how parents brought a strong diversity of literacies that incorporated different identities and narratives. Taylor argued that these narratives should be used to tell schools how to teach literacy (Taylor, 1983).

In many research studies, there has been evidence that has backed up Taylor's findings and has helped educators appreciate the complex literacy practices children engage in at home (Compton-Lilly & Greene, 2011). For example, Heath's study of the literacy practices of three different communities in the Carolinas helped us to understand different patterns in literacy practices from school patterns (Heath, 1983). There have been fewer studies of multilingual children's text-making at home. Kenner's study of bilingual children revealed many different sorts of texts being produced by children at home, including word searches, cards and letters (Kenner, 2000). Studies of children's popular culture and literacy found that many children responded to the videos and games they played with, incorporating dance, songs and stories (Marsh & Thompson, 2001). New forms of literacy are now prevalent in homes, as many studies (for example, Marsh, 2005) attest.

NEW TECHNOLOGIES IN THE HOME GOING TO SCHOOL

A key area for educators is the impact of new technologies in the home. In a teacher-research project, Susan Hill explored young children's use of new technologies at home as well as in pre-schools and schools. She wanted to know what were the different ways that young children used literacy at home and in the community, and how these were different at home and at school. She developed a framework for teachers to describe children's use of multimodal texts (Hill, 2010). She opened up a shared discourse about how teachers could use new literacies in school. In the project, conducted in Australia, teacher-researchers visited 48 homes and asked children to take them on a 'technotour' to find out what kinds of new technologies could be found in the home. They explored, with young children, ways in which new multimodal texts could be constructed using these new forms of literacy. They used this experience to create

> ... a shared discourse about how texts operate or function, the meanings they make, ways to critically analyse or deconstruct texts and then transforming existing texts into new forms. (Hill, 2010: 337)

The merging of new and old forms of literacy in multimodal texts is a way forward for teachers to make sense of new technologies in the classroom. Julia Davies and Guy Merchant, in their book on Web 2 for schools, provide a number of examples of children and young people using *Twitter*, *YouTube*, blogs and virtual worlds in literacy learning contexts (Davies & Merchant, 2009). Jackie Marsh has written about using

Club Penguin with young children to support literacy learning (Marsh, 2011). Children's online selves and identities are powerful tools to use in classroom literacy learning.

Vignette: Making sense of new online games

The new space of online games as educational tools for literacy learning has also been explored by Eve Bearne and Cary Bazalgette in their book, *Beyond Words: Developing Children's Response to Multimodal Texts* (2010), in which children were encouraged to critically respond to multimedia texts, including online games. For example, in a school in Sheffield, a group of 5- to 6-year-olds played an online game. They found that in order to progress through the levels, it was important to access written information as well as the icons. The discussion they had after playing the game reflected the need to understand the structure of hyperlinks, and the literacy embedded within these structures, to 'do' the game successfully. Here, a teacher is prepared to engage with online games as a particular form of literacy. The teacher reflected.

> In addition to the pictures and verbal clues, there are 'special' words or pictures – the hyperlinks that for many children override any decisions about what information to focus on in a web page. Added to that, the reading direction of the screen is different from a book. The information, unlike in most traditional texts, is not presented linearly (left to right) but rather spatially and without convention. A hyperlink can be anywhere on a page and in pictorial or text form. ... Web pages come with their own unique set of motivational drives for children ... .
> (Winter, 2010, writing in Bearne, & Bazalgette, 2010: 15–16)

The teacher, Peter Winter, concluded that it was important to develop in children the ability to make sense of this process and to focus with them on how to access the games most successfully, using a multimodal approach to instruction.

In the examples above, teachers are using new literacies to link home and school. New literacies, in the form of blogs, wikis, online games, social networking pages and sites as well as other kinds of digital meaning-making, such as digital storytelling and film making, can provide opportunities for children and young people to merge home experiences and funds of knowledge with content area literacy from school. These forms of linkages can be made in visual, oral and gestural modes as well as in language. Opening out the affordances of multimodal meaning-making to the digital can let in many other kinds of meanings.

LEARNING FROM FAMILIES

Learning from families requires a particular listening methodology that can then involve change. It opens up a new space in the classroom.

- How can educators draw on these examples to improve their practice?

In much of the work on children's out-of-school literacies, there is a recognition of how children blend a number of different forms, and draw on different ways of making-meaning when they make texts. Dyson calls this process 'remix' and applied it in her work to the children she observed who mixed rap songs and nursery rhymes in their out-of-school practices (Dyson, 2003). It is the *relational* power of pedagogy that can link home literacies to school contexts. Eve Bearne writes that:

> Rethinking literacy requires a pedagogy which can accommodate to children's situated text experience brought from the everyday world of communications and relate this both to the schooled literacy of the classroom situation and to the institutional practices which shape current practice. (Bearne, 2003: 102)

This means that when we think about children's text-making, we consider all the influences that come into their lives. In this chapter, we suggest that children's text-making at home and at school needs to become more 'joined up'. When linking up home and school the variety of children's popular cultural worlds needs to be considered. An 'asset' model can be applied, which acknowledges these influences as assets in the development of children's meaning-making. When children's texts go to school they can be readily comprehended and supported.

CONCLUSION

This chapter has described home literacy, using a range of studies drawing on methodologies such as ethnography and visual methods, and how it can be moved into schools. It has looked at a range of approaches to the development of children's literacy at school. It has considered the ways in which different programmes have supported children's literacy, and their different cultural worlds. This chapter offers some directions for educators. It suggests that '... educators learn to listen to students' writing lives and incorporate their students' out-of-school literacy practices into a permeable curriculum (Schultz, 2002: 386).

This perspective gives educators the challenge of:

- finding out about the literacy practices of their students;

- sharing them in a community of practice with the class;

- building on these practices in classroom settings.

Classrooms of the future may incorporate the ways in which homes work. At home, movement across sites and across modes may be happening much more quickly, and to a different timeframe from that at school. We need to examine what literacy activities our students are engaging with out of school, and consider how we can form bridges to support students within school. This will give us the opportunity to think more clearly about what literacy is being supported where.

In addition, we need to pay attention to the complex blend of new and old media which is central to the experience of the everyday cultures of childhood and adolescence (Carrington, 2005). Like it or not, textual practices such as email, social networking sites, blogs, online shopping, webcams, messaging and games using **avatars** online are part of young people's realities. **It is time to take these forms into our schools and use them.**

Literacies in the community

Vignette: Garden as text – cultivating knowledge between parents and their children

By Saskia Stille

Sabil is a 9-year-old boy who has recently immigrated to a large city in Canada. Like many of his classmates, he lives in a high-rise apartment building close to his new school. Sabil's Grade 3 class had recently begun to study the curricular topic of urban and rural communities, providing a rich opportunity to connect with students' authentic social realities. Sabil described: 'I had a garden in Afghanistan. My grandfather worked with me in my garden.' Another student shared her experience: 'We had a big farm in our country. I miss the flowers, the smell.' Because the students and their families now lived in apartment buildings, they had few opportunities to draw upon these experiences in their new Canadian home. For these reasons, together we decided to create an edible school garden.

To prepare for this project, we engaged the students in researching issues of food and sustainability. Working with partners, students chose a topic of interest and prepared a PowerPoint presentation to display their findings. Sabil and his partner decided to find out 'Where Bread Comes From', learning about planting, farming, and producing wheat. Integrating web-based content into their research, the students used the class computers to search for digital images to accompany the information they found from books in the school library.

Students also used the class computers to write letters to businesses who donated equipment and supplies for the garden, including shovels, spades, bags of soil, plants, and seeds.

(Cont'd)

Moving our work outdoors, the students mapped the area for the garden. The location available to us had been unused and was completely covered with long grass and weeds. Recognizing the great deal of work ahead of us, as well as the experiences of the students' families in farming, we invited parents to work with us in the garden. Working side by side, the students and their parents put in long hours to prepare the ground by hand. We tilled soil, planted seeds, watered, and weeded. After a long summer, we enjoyed the products of this labour – melons, pumpkins, carrots, sunflowers, and tea brewed from the herbs we had grown.

The school garden provided access to land on which parents and their children could grow flowers, plants, or vegetables. Hamza's father commented, 'If you don't understand about agriculture, you don't understand where your food comes from, what people are doing for you.'

As a mode of communication, the garden was a text through which parents passed on to their children their knowledge and experience of working the land. The garden unearthed topics and subject-matter knowledge that were previously unavailable for learning in the school. Rupturing and remaking the school space, the garden enabled students and their families to contribute to the construction and production of curriculum knowledge in (and outside!) the classroom.

Key themes in the chapter:

- Researching literacy practices in homes and communities
- Ecological literacies
- Multilingual literacies
- Local and global literacies
- Spatial literacies

INTRODUCTION

Literacies in community contexts are nested within the cultural, economic and social forces that surround them. In poor neighbourhoods, literacy is often less visible as shops are closed down, and resources are withheld due to economic constraints (Neuman & Celano, 2001). Local literacies are linked to the sounds, the accents and the smells of the neighbourhoods. Reading the community is about reading the social worlds of the children brought up in the neighbourhood. It is also about the layered nature of experience and the ways in which children come to know the world. In this chapter, the focus will be on ecological approaches to literacy. By 'ecological' we mean that in any community there is an ecology of literacy. Literacies circulate in local spaces such as health centres, libraries, schools, youth clubs, and community centres as well as in homes and in the street. Literacy can be linked and understood as a web of practices. These practices can be drawn on by children as they make meaning in school. Literacies can also be more abundant in some areas than in others. There is an inequality around the availability of literacies across neighbourhoods. As we see below, from Neuman and Celano's work (2001), some neighbourhoods are more literacy-rich than others. Some neighbourhoods also carry literacies that are negative, such as offensive or racist graffiti, and the work of the researcher of literacy practices is to problematize this. In this chapter, we draw on the work of Bill Green to see literacy as both *cultural*, that is, embedded in contexts, *critical*, that is, as a source of power relations and also a site of critique, and also *operational*, that is, as something to be learned (Green, 1998).

 Activity

Mapping the Neighbourhood

Draw a map of your neighbourhood. Think about the key sites or hubs for literacy. Where does literacy take place? Where are the valued literacies and where are the ephemeral literacies? Which literacy practices matter to you?

Now consider the neighbourhood from a child's perspective and consider how literacy looks from their perspective. Does it look different? How is literacy experienced by a child in a stroller or buggy? By a 5-year-old? Or a 10-year-old? Imagine literacy from the point of view of the home, the street and then the school. What does it look like?

Finally, use your map to list as an inventory all the literacy practices in your area. How many do you locate in the school or institutional context and how many do you locate in an informal setting?

In this chapter, we explore the location of literacies and make sense of communities in relation to literacy. We take literacy out into the streets, into public parks, into social everyday spaces, where groups of people move and where literacy is sometimes embedded, sometimes invisible.

- What can a view of literacy that takes in place and space offer literacy education?

Vignette: Writing in the home and in the street

I (Kate) was able to conduct a research project with a group of Year 6 children from a Junior School alongside their class teacher. The area where we worked was marked by the economic downturn and had high levels of socio-economic deprivation. We wanted to focus on literacy in the area. In order to find out about the literacy practices in the area we planned a session on writing in the community. We asked the students to brainstorm their writing practices in the home, the school, and write these up on a chart. The children start to describe the writing they see in their home. This began to map the community's writing practices. From the chart, we talked about the different writing practices found in the home, the street and school, and started to develop a research project with the children. They could then document the writing practices in the home and community. Then the children researched community literacies by doing community walk-arounds using still and video cameras. Students created a film about the literacy that goes on in the school, their homes and community. They recorded the walk-arounds on film and on audio. Their message was to examine, sometimes critically, the literacies they found across community contexts. In some cases, the literacies were problematic. The children found that some of the graffiti they recorded was offensive for young children. The children also interviewed the local police officer and were able to effect change – the police officer said he would work with the children to get rid of the offensive graffiti in the community. Luke said this about the graffiti he photographed:

Kate: I want to know what you think of the graffiti on this slide?

Luke: It's all rude! We should spray it. It's not fair on young children.

(Community walk-around audio, June 2011)

Figure 4.1   Photographing community literacies

In the vignette on the previous page, the children created a shift in the literacies in the community through documenting literacy practices in communities. We argue in this chapter that if literacies in communities are understood, they can then inform the way we teach and describe literacy more clearly in the classroom.

UNDERSTANDING ECOLOGIES OF LITERACY IN COMMUNITIES

Children bring themselves to the texts they read and make, and their identities inform the meaning-making process. Children's experience of literacy is built up by their experiences of community, of home and neighbourhoods. Children walk to school in neighbourhoods that are filled with artifacts that signal literacy.

- Name one community artifact around your school and speak with your students about this artifact.

Literacy is experienced 'from the feet up' in Margaret Mackey's words, and this experience is sensory and embodied (Pink, 2009; Mackey, 2010). Communities are where literacy is, on doors, on lamp-posts, in store fronts, and in the form of signage and leaflets. The holistic linking of places, spaces, people, and the artifacts that matter to them is repre-sented on the next page, in Figure 4.2.

The outermost layer is place as in a regional area of study, such as New Jersey; the second layer is particular towns and districts with their own specificities, such as the town of Princeton. This can be seen in a holistic way, as an ecology, that is, something connected through visible and invisible threads that are co-dependent. An ecological perspective takes from science a focus on people's reliance on resources to access and mobilize different parts of a community in day-to-day life and how this impacts on identities (Neuman & Celano, 2001). Within an ecology of literacy, there are hubs of activity, such as libraries and community cen-tres, or faith groups, where people meet and congregate and where local practices and common texts circulate. Finally, nested within place, ecol-ogy, and hubs are literacy practices as expressions of space, place, beliefs, thoughts, subjectivities, and stories that accompany each one. Literacy practices exist within a web of activity and hubs. For example, a special artwork, *Happy World* existed inside a public library in Princeton, US, which in turn, was nested within the hub that was the town of Princeton. This town was in turn within New Jersey, a state in the United States. By seeing *Happy World*, the art project, in context, its spatial dimensions can

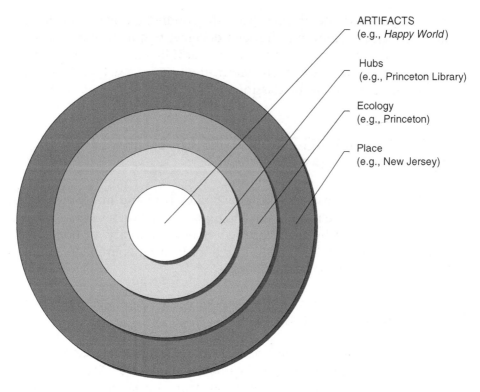

ARTIFACTS
(e.g., *Happy World*)

Hubs
(e.g., Princeton Library)

Ecology
(e.g., Princeton)

Place
(e.g., New Jersey)

Figure 4.2 Neighbourhood hubs

be appreciated. The artwork, a collection of tiles made by local people, became an instantiation of the neighbourhood and the ways in which people made sense of their home town.

The chapter considers how to use an ecological approach to literacy in classroom practice. At the beginning of the chapter we heard about the idea of garden-as-text and the construction of literacies from a community project. We also heard about how a group of children researched literacy in a school and in the community. This chapter builds on Chapter 3, with its emphasis on family literacies informing school literacy teaching; the crossing of sites is an important area of inquiry and thought for literacy teachers.

Local classroom contexts are tied to ecological spaces as well as global contexts. Just as literacy events and practices are bound to classroom contexts, to teachers and to students, so too, local-based practices and assumptions are bound to the other links that children have within the community. Children attend health clinics, visit local libraries, belong to youth clubs and attend churches and after-school mosque class. They learn community languages in complementary schools (Blackledge & Creese, 2010). Their experience of early literacy is situated by their experience of neighbourhood.

Theory Box: Susan Neuman and Donna Celano take an ecological approach to literacy practices

Neuman and Celano (2001, 2006) conducted a number of studies in Philadephia investigating four neighbourhoods in terms of the opportunities offered for children and their families to engage in literacy-related activities. Their method involved walking through a block of each neighbourhood and noting stores, signage, neighbourhood hubs and places generally where reading could be undertaken, and relevant institutional sites (libraries, child care centres, etc.) available to residents. What they found was that neighbourhoods of different socio-economic status showed striking differences in terms of access to literacy resources and opportunities. Neuman and Celano established a method for gathering ecological data to explore the affordances of certain neighbourhoods over others for information sourcing.

By seeing literacies as ecologies, out-of-school literacy practices matter as the spaces where young people do literacy. Educators need to honour these experiences as important because they are seen through young peoples' eyes. Below, a group of young people consider the role of literacy in their community library.

Vignette: A group of young people make a film about literacy in a library

The initial research focus for the study was to explore why young people attended a particular library after school and, in particular, how they viewed literacy within the site. The library was a new-build library situated in a deprived area in a town in the North of England. Drawing on Neuman and Celano (2006), we (Kate and Chloe Allan) started from their insight that, 'libraries are not primary spaces but optional ones that are visited rather than inhabited' (2006: 181). We wanted to know what the library meant to a group of young people who visited it regularly. The children and young people using the space did not seem, for the majority, to associate

(Cont'd)

words like library and literacy with books and reading. For them the library is a place to see friends and literacy is something 'for other people'. We observed, however, lots of reading being done within the library, such as:

- using computers;

- typing on MSN and *Facebook*;

- the words on the coffee machine;

- signage;

- posters;

- word search puzzles;

- children's magazines, etc.

We were interested in these informal literacies and what the children thought of them.

Because our research question focused on what the library offered in terms of literacy for the young people who used it, we needed to focus on the environment. We argued from a methodological perspective, that a participatory, ecological methodology could open up a new research space which might also bring agency into the picture, as the young people in the study actively planned and delivered the research. Participatory research with children has grown with the use of visual and reflective methodologies that engage children seriously with the research process.

Clark, Kjorholt and Moss (2005) use the 'Mosaic Approach' to involve children in the production and analysis of images, maps and other oral and linguistic texts that listen to children in an active way to transform children's

Fieldnotes by two researchers	Treasure island activity done by young people	Disposable cameras sent home with young people to record literacy practices	Interviews with library users constructed and filmed by young people on FLIP cameras
Leaflet collection by researchers	Ecological study in a community library		Use of FLIP cameras to record community walk-around by young people
Interviews with librarians by researchers	Use of photographs by researchers of community	Use of photographs by young of library	Scrapbooks of images, thoughts and impressions by young people

Figure 4.3 The range of methods used in the study

spaces through architecture. In this research project, we drew on a number of visual methods as, led by the children, we explored meanings and practices on site, in a situated and embedded methodological space.

This led on to a participatory research project with a group of children aged between 6 and 12, called 'Research Rebels' (February–May 2010). The project continued with interviews with key people in the library by the children, a community walk-around with the children, discussion and analysis of the FLIP video camera dataset, together with further films of library activity. We followed this by giving the children disposable cameras to record literacy practices in the home, which they then placed in scrapbooks to represent their home and community literacies. The focus of the study was on:

- What did the library mean to us?

- How do the children use the library?

- How is literacy relevant for the children and where is it present in the library?

- Where is literacy in the community?

However, we realized that we needed to look at literacy from the perspective of the children. In the final stage of the project, the children jointly produced a film about the library. This was shown to a senior member of the library service, at a community showing at the end of the project (Pahl & Allan, 2011).

The implications of attending to an ecological perspective is that learning is situated, collaborative and shared. It is focused on sites and spaces for learning. To illustrate what this means, let's return to the vignette at the beginning of the chapter. Thinking about this text, it was a collaborative project and the mode of the text was the garden. The garden was a site for the learning processes and steps taken by the children and parents to remake meaning. The audience of the text was the students and families, and by remaking the school space, the function of the text-as-garden enabled students and their families to contribute to the construction and production of curriculum knowledge in (and outside!) the classroom. The concept of garden as text also widens our understanding of the ways in which different kinds of spaces are textually mediated.

This form of inquiry looks beyond the practical in our language and literacy teaching to understand what shared ideas lie beneath our texts, our practices, our understandings, and our assumptions. How we make meaning is tied to where and within what communities, forms of knowledge, and underlying meanings we read and we write. The New Literacy Studies looks at *literacy as a social practice*. In doing so, the theories then take account of the ecological spaces around meaning-making. Ecological literacies mean that we need to take account of our students' everyday identities. This puts the focus back on to meaning, the ways in which some students carry their narratives of migration with them across contexts, into new settings and new cultural identities.

 Activity

Mapping Home Objects as Sites for Literacy

Make an inventory of objects in your home that carry print. How many contain hidden literacies, either in the form of instruction manuals or fleeting ephemeral print. Continue to log print in online and offline literacy practices as you encounter different leisure activities. Where can literacy be framed as 'print' and where is it framed as something else, such as craft or image?

Consider how you could link these embedded or invisible literacies to classroom activities. Create a template that charts the original practice and then link it to a genre or text type. For example, a message on a piece of embroidery could be translated into letter writing.

Vignette: A home as a site for literacy

When I enter this home, which is a family of British-Asian heritage, in an industrial Northern town in the UK, these are the forms of writing I note. I drive my car up a narrow street of Victorian terraced houses, although this particular house I am to visit happens to be detached. I get out of my car, and walk up to the front porch. Over the door to the house, itself a late-Victorian detached house, built about 1901, is the name of the house inscribed in plaster on the outside. This was written in the early years of the late twentieth century and is fixed, being inscribed in a stone-like substance. As I enter, there are framed, small, inscriptions over the doors, which are written in Arabic, as they relate to sections of the Quran and signify holy words. These inscriptions are also fixed. They were put up when they first came to the house, in December 2010. The family describe themselves as British-Asian Muslims. They therefore see the inscriptions as important to provide holy texts for their home.

I walk into the back of the house, where there is a fireplace, and a computer and two sofas to sit on. The family have three children; one aged 2 years of age, one of 8 and one of 12, all girls. When I walk in, the things on the floor and on the seating area vary. Sometimes there are toys and small books. There are to be found fragments of script within the toys and artifacts strewn about the floor of the back living room. For example, a board book for the youngest was inscribed with Arabic letters. Most recently, I encountered an 'Etch-a-Sketch', on which the youngest writes. These objects are relatively fluid in that they move about and are sometimes visible and sometimes tidied away when the youngest is asleep and the mother does the housework. A computer is placed in the corner, on which the older girls do their homework and write stories and emails to me, and the mother sends orders for garden products. I can observe some fixed and settled forms of writing (writing on the house, inscription on the framed images, the computer with the sign of the maker) and some less fixed forms of writing, including those that are fixed but put away (toy laptop, books, drawing materials) and some that are never permanent (the lines made by the child in her 'Etch-a-Sketch').

Within this space, script is present, but it is not always fixed. It flows throughout the household. Sometimes it is momentarily fixed, as the girls bring in a cloth bag with script embroidered on it, or the family might decide to consult *Street View* to look at neighbouring streets. Stories and coloured-in writing are found within the home and presented to me as examples of script that the girls produce at home. Script is often ephemerally located and flows within family life. These forms of writing are not often recognizable as the writing forms located within schooling. The writing I watch in the home is linked to the epistemologies of those who created it, to the builder who marked the house, to the person who made the Arabic inscription which was then purchased and displayed like a picture in the home, to the momentary trace of writing by the 2-year-old on the 'Etch-a-Sketch', to the coloured stitches of the eldest as she embroiders her bag. Each of these forms of writing was contained within an epistemological space. The writing is also linked to other spaces – the sewing club where the bag was written, to the library where the colouring activities took place.

This vignette takes account of the spaces of literacy practices as well as the links between offline and online literacies. Literacy practices are linked across by invisible lines to other spaces and contexts. This provides the ecologies of writing. Some of this writing takes place between contexts or on route to other settings. It also takes account of the family's intergenerational literacy practices, and the different literacies in the families, from the craft literacies, to the inscriptions on the wall and to the play literacies strewn in the toys about the house. Literacy in this home is always on the move and is always subject to cultural change. It is an example of what Brian Street called 'Culture is a Verb' (Street, 1993a).

Theory Box: Sue Nichols, Helen Nixon and Jennifer Rowsell on parents' networks of information about children's literacy and language development

Building on the research of scholars such as Neuman and Celano, Sue Nichols, Helen Nixon and Jennifer Rowsell conducted a three-year, multi-sited project examining parents' networks of information about children's literacy and language development. They used a similar ecological survey approach to study neighbourhood hubs and differentials in access to resources. Nichols et al. combine an ecological survey with geosemiotics and network theory. The research team examined resources used by families to support children's early learning that are located in geographic space. Even Internet access points (including wireless hotspots) are physically located. Their study offers an innovative methodology that can be built on by other researchers doing ecological work (Nichols et al., 2009; Nichols, 2011).

ECOLOGICAL TEXTS AS MULTIMODAL

As noted in earlier chapters, meaning is made in ways that are increasingly multimodal, whereby written, that is linguistic, modes of meaning work in sync. with the visual, the audio, and spatial patterns of meaning. For example, in Chapter 2, we saw how literacy was tied to the 'spin' of production. This kind of ecological work is new to this second edition of *Literacy and Education*. These systems are multimodal. Most of our communication systems rely on multimodality to create a message. Using a multimodal approach to understanding text production in communities can lead to the following questions:

• What is the collaborative community/learning process embedded in the content of texts?

• What is the intended audience of a text?

• What is the function of a text?

• What is the mode of the text?

• Was the text produced locally in a community context or globally?

Given that the substance, content and aesthetics of multimodality rely on the ethos of the ecological, which relies on an understanding of community, we should account for community in our meaning-making.

We therefore need to research literacies in communities in our quest for an ecological understanding of community. Moje (2000) suggests that the concept of community needs to be understood not as a reified fact, but as something complex, contested and alive with problematics. Children perceive the neighbourhoods in which they live from particular, situated perspectives that may differ from those of adults. Studies such as those by Christiansen and O'Brien (2003) and Orellana (1999) have involved asking children to represent their social worlds through images, in interaction and through walking around the community with the researchers. Children come at their experience bodily, through their own eyes. Ethnography and cultural geography provide situated accounts of children and adults' experience of place and space and the body (Christiansen & O'Brien, 2003; Pink, 2009). The garden vignette at the beginning of the chapter shows us the ways in which identities are inextricably interwoven with place. Neighbourhood and the local community are where children first encounter others, and it is in these encounters that literacy practices emerge and take shape, over time.

MULTILINGUAL LITERACIES

Children also work across scripts and within and across languages. The ecologies of literacy mean paying attention to the multilingual as well as the multimodal. Blackledge and Creese (2010) describe how children use digital equipment such as texting and MP3 file sharing quite naturally, and embed their language with diverse linguistic practices. By combining the digital with the multilingual and multimodal, it is possible to see how children's literacies are situated differently in community contexts.

Theory Box: Adrian Blackledge and Angela Creese on multilingual literacies

In their study of complementary schools in four different language settings (Turkish, Chinese, Urdu and Hindi), a group of multilingual researchers explored how linguistic practices were connected to popular cultural practices inside and outside class, and how the use of artifacts such as mobile phones facilitated file sharing of different music files in the classroom, as a popular cultural literacy practice. They argue that multilingual literacies in these classrooms need to be understood as complex, fluid and meshed with other practices. They use the term 'translanguaging' to describe this process. An ecological approach takes account of these meshed linguistic practices (Blackledge & Creese, 2010).

In urban classrooms, where there are students from a variety of cultures, who speak a variety of languages at home, and at school and on the street, there are ways of respecting cultural practices within the curriculum, through a multimodal approach, such as in drama, in role-play, in music, in computers, and through the arts. For example, a Tile Project took place in a Turkish community in a school in North London. Its aim was to encourage children to work on their drawings of plants in science and turn them into Turkish tiles – linking science and the arts.

- How can you link subject areas through a multimodal approach?

An ecological approach to literacy implies an understanding of the power relations around literacy. An ecological approach has and does supply a context for different kinds of research on literacy. An example of different kinds of research is to look at language. How we speak in one local context can be quite different from a neighbouring local context. Comparing and contrasting language use in the two contexts helps us to understand complex sets of values, beliefs and agendas. Language – how and when it is used – separates one society from the next. Such theorizing leads to a belief in the situated nature of language. Language practices can change to meet local conditions.

If we are to understand the relationship between communities and literacy, we need to understand how the cultural background of our students relates to classroom practice. This situated approach can explore how texts are created from students' home and community experiences and their transnational experiences.

When we scaffold our students' home culture and social practices within their schooling contexts, students are able to situate themselves in the process. They can find themselves in the ecological spaces of home and community and embed their identities in artifacts such as a poem or a digital image. That is, they can bring a part of themselves tied to family and their birthplace and recreate it in a contemporary medium. After all, children are the masters of our new communicational systems and by combining them with more traditional methods, we are speaking to their needs and to their interests.

ECOLOGICAL LITERACIES AND GLOBAL CONTEXTS

Deborah Brandt and Katie Clinton, in their article 'The Limits of the Local', explore the evolution of the New Literacy Studies, discussing studies that led to literacy as a social practice as a framework (Brandt &

Clinton, 2002). Formerly, many literacy theorists and educators adopted a *cognitive* model of literacy development, whereby we carry language skills with us and it is through teaching and usage that we become literate. In the work of Brandt and Clinton, they maintain that *social context* organizes literacy as opposed to literacy organizing social context.

In an *autonomous model of literacy*, as discussed in Chapter 1, texts dictate terms for the reader, whereas in an *ideological model of literacy*, the reader and the context dictate the terms of how a text is read and understood. Such a shift in thinking gives more power to the reader and the context as carriers of their own meanings, discourses and ideologies. We understand all of this as being part of the theories described within the New Literacy Studies. What has not been accounted for as much is the relationship between local practices and their tie to the ecological and to **globalization.** Just as Discourses exist within discourses, so too Cultures (to take up Gee's use of upper and lower case) exist within cultures. If we locate the way we embed our ecologies' culture and our history into our literacy teaching and learning, and equally, the way students embed their ecologies of culture and history into their literacy learning, we are that much closer to understanding where our literacy skills and assumptions end and where ecological influences begin. As Carol Lee (2008) has said, 'culture matters' and the ecologies of families also matter. For example, in the vignette of the family above, they were able to communicate with family members in Pakistan at the same time as looking at their new house, in a local area, on *Street View*.

Theory Box: Deborah Brandt and Katie Clinton on the local and the global

Deobrah Brandt and Katie Clinton (2002) argue that detailed ethnographic studies which demonstrate the role of identity and context in language development need to be located within a larger, global framework. If we regard *literacy as a global and social practice*, we have to analyze how we communicate across cultures within a global space. Brandt and Clinton draw from the work of Bruno Latour (1996) in arguing for a local–global continuum within a literacy framework. Latour speaks of an Ariadne's thread that allows us to pass seamlessly from the local to the global (Brandt & Clinton, 2002).

The local and the global rely on each other and manifest themselves in our objects, in our speech, and in our practices. There is an increasing nexus between what goes on locally and what goes on globally. There is a thread of networks and practices that cuts across cultures, sites, **communities of practice,** and identities in practice that can be traced. For example, Helen Nixon (2011) looked at how parenting manuals were constructed globally but experienced locally in her study of literacies in shopping malls aimed at constructing the idea of the 'good parent'.

- Can you identify texts that you use on a daily basis that are both local and global?

Websites can be understood as being constructed drawing on local and global texts (Sheridan & Rowsell, 2010). Every text and practice bears traces of former texts and practices. However, studying literacy from strictly inside the frame (i.e., strictly from a local perspective), global contexts get lost or blurred. According to Brandt and Clinton (2002), it is vital to look simultaneously at local and **global literacies** and observe how they play out in everyday practices. For example, students could consider banking practices from the point of view of the local economy but also discuss the way in which global forces have shaped this local economy. These links can be used when coming to understand the ecologies of literacy in communities.

ECOLOGIES OF MULTILINGUAL LITERACIES

By welcoming the linguistic resources students bring to class, language learners are placed within contexts that acknowledge what they have to offer within a classroom setting. An ecological approach sees languages and literacies as diverse. Multiple literacies involve several different language varieties and scripts, complex and multiple repertoires that can be documented through ethnographic observation. That is, these same linguistic differences and visual and oral repertoires are carried over into different communicative events. For example, when we move from a school setting to a commercial setting like a department store or shopping mall, we are still using language varieties and scripts, and the same can be said when we travel across settings. In many everyday contexts, dual languages are common. Walking along a street in a multilingual community can elicit studies of the languages spoken in that community and the scripts employed (Collins, Slembrouck & Baynham, 2009).

Children acquire home languages at different rates, and acquire different language systems using different ways of instruction. Eve Gregory has documented how Bangladeshi children learn Arabic using very different pedagogical models from the way they acquire or develop their English in schools (Gregory, 2008).

In our speaking, in our listening, and in our actions, there is a mixing and melding together of different voices, which form a mix of our communicative repertoires. Theorists in the area of New Literacy Studies speak of **hybridity** in this light: as a blending of linguistic repertoires and accompanying practices within situated speech.

Theory Box: Eve Gregory, Susi Long and Diana Volk on syncretic literacies

Researchers such as Eve Gregory, Susi Long and Dinah Volk found that children blend literacy practices. These literacy practices come from:

- home;

- school;

- popular culture;

- religion;

- community groups (Volk, 1997).

Volk described the complex web of continuities and discontinuities in language use patterns of 5-year-olds. Volk argued that parents speaking to their children at home insert patterns of interaction from school into home practices. These intergenerational language and literacy practices are situated within a complex web of community and familial relationships that link to ecological literacies (Gregory et al., 2004).

In everyday life, we mix popular culture texts with long-standing community and social practices and traditions. There is a rich vein of inquiry and relevance to language teaching when we account for complex mixes of cultural traditions within our speech patterns. Appreciating the local and the global, and the local cultural identity of our students, opens up opportunities for richer classroom experiences. Many researchers have located the intersection of culture and new media and its impact on language.

- Can you locate local media (e.g., local newspaper) and global media (e.g., international paper)?

As new migrant families arrive in neighbourhoods, their textual practices might change, as letters are sent home, and the family might use a number of different multilingual literacy practices in different settings (Saxena, 2000). They might attend school in English and mosque school in Arabic, and use the Urdu script to write letters home, while conversing in Punjabi or similar as specific languages connected to place. These multilingual literacy practices might remain the same in some domains, but be stretched in others. For example, a family arriving from Somalia might carry with them Arabic literacy practices tied to the local mosque, which involves attending a mosque school and learning by heart the holy Quran in Arabic, a practice that might be invisible in schooling (Gregory, Long & Volk, 2004; Rosowsky, 2008). Children might then draw on these decoding skills when learning to read in schools (Rosowsky, 2001).

 Points of Reflection: Neighbourhoods as sites of super diversity

If you walk in any major city (from Cape Town to Montreal to Mumbai to Melbourne to Nairobi), script is present in its linguistic diversity and multi-modality. Urban sites are good spaces to trace the ecologies of **multilingualism**. It is then possible to locate 'contact zones' (Pratt, 1992) where languages are present alongside each other and are in communication with each other. These spaces offer a hybrid, multi-voiced linguistic cultural space. Children growing up in these neighbourhoods experience the range of languages as a landscape of diverse voices, scripts and images. Visiting a major city can involve tracing the 'contact zones' where languages connect and sometimes co-exist alongside each other, given equal prominence on signs and streets.

SPATIAL APPROACHES TO LITERACY

We draw on the work of Comber, Thomson and Wells (2001) and consider how students' sense of place can be developed as a pedagogical approach, as here:

> Marg's students take possession of their neighborhood by walking around in it, by exploring its nooks and secret places, by finding favorite places. (Comber et al., 2001: 461)

When we think about ecologies of literacy, we think about space. We consider the landscape in which our students live. While we have considered urban contexts in this chapter, it is also important to consider rural spaces. A rural literacies approach focuses on the importance of landscape and environment as a resource for meaning-making and as a site of resilience (Brooke, 2003; Corbett, 2007). Barbara Comber works with teachers to think about the spaces students grow up in to acknowledge the importance of recognizing the streets and neighbourhoods as resources for literacy (Comber, 2010). This might mean creating new spaces for meaning-making through community photography and drawing, and using this to create writing opportunities. When teachers hear about the spaces students inhabit, we learn how to listen and to make space for the stories they tell about those spaces.

- Where are the salient spaces in your community for literacy for different age ranges – for children, for teenagers, for elderly people?

In the section that follows, consider how space and place can be used as resources for meaning-making within classroom contexts. Drawing on the work of Comber (2010), we think about ways of creating spaces that draw on place-based literacies to develop their own writing practices. Massey (2005) talks about the 'thrown togetherness' of places, in that students are placed in different kinds of spaces and then have to make meaning collaboratively in the classroom. Soja (2010) described how people need to have control over their geographies. A spatial justice approach to literacy creates new ways for people to articulate and change the spaces they inhabit. In this second edition, the field has moved on in terms of space and place-based work and this shift is signalled in the next section.

INSCRIBING PLACE AND SPACE THROUGH TEXT-MAKING

How do students connect their worlds of home, community, and school – both the continuities and discontinuities? Children growing up in neighbourhoods experience the textual and artifactual nature of the space into which they are born. Their lives are meshed with the experience of the neighbourhood, its boundaries and its lived experiences. Walking through neighbourhoods, children experience their worlds in a sensory way, through smell, sound and sight. These experiences are translated into texts, into writing, talk, and pictures.

Communities are increasingly recognized as being about place, about social networks and, most meaningful, about interaction. Interaction consists of oral storytelling, but also involves the production of written as well as oral texts between people within communities.

Place has often been seen as a more bounded, physical concept, whereas space can be associated with the virtual and the non-physical. Leander and Sheehy (2004) argue that discursive practices produce new kinds of spaces, and, particularly in virtual worlds, Gee (2003) in his work on videogames pushed this further to describe how new spaces are then co-constructed online. However, discursive practices themselves are always open to interpretation. Experience is something that is acquired over time, and people's memories shift as they grow up. Family myths emerge over time as part of a collective memory; however, the myths we live by are themselves constructed in interaction (Connerton, 1989; Samuel & Thompson, 1990). The experience of space involves oscillation between memories of a place, embodied experience of place, and then the construction of new spaces through interaction. This process leads to literacy.

Vignette: A child finds safety in meaning-making

Lucy, aged 12, was of Pakistani heritage, living in a Northern town in the UK. She and her parents and two sisters had recently moved from a place where they felt unsafe to a much safer street, where the family had relatives. Her mother reflected on the move, and said that the move had taken her back to her family. The children told me (Kate) how they had experienced racism in the old area, including a break-in of their family home. However, the girls adopted coping strategies. Lucy's sister talked about her ambition to be an explorer when she grew up. Lucy wrote letters to reassure the self who got lost and felt scared:

Dear Agony Aunt

My name is Stella.

Tomorrow is my first day in comprehensive. I am really worried that I will get lost and I would get into so much trouble. I have never got into any trouble before with both school and home. What should I do if get lost? Please help! Stella X

Dear Stella.

Don't worry.

Everyone gets lost on their first day. It took me a whole week to know where all my classes were. I was very worried myself that I would get lost. But I just asked a teacher, a pupil or just had a look around if there are no teachers or pupils around. You will be okay. All the best.
Agony Aunt

The girls began to explore their new space, and as they did so, they described the safety they felt in their new home. The younger sister, Tanya, described her experience of the new house:

I am going to see my grandad's house, my grandma's there and then there is next door neighbour and next door neighbour and next door neighbour and then it's our house it's a blue one and it's all ruined. (Audio recording, November 22, 2010)

The family's new house was slowly renovated, and, on the outside of the house, a diamond shape was made that, to the younger sister, represented the different people in her family. She felt safe in the new house, and her literacy practices reflected that sense of safety.

CONCLUSION

What lies at the heart of this chapter is a focus on literacies as circulating across a range of spaces. Children both draw their strength from these literacies and also can critique them. Children bring their ecologies and their cultural practices as well as multilingual and multimodal literacies into primary classrooms and find their way into language and into print from a specific ecological and cultural lens which guides their literacy practices. Their voices need to be heard to influence community literacy strategy.

How can these ideas be used in the classroom? Many practitioners working within a New Literacy Studies framework would argue that effective literacy learning in current educational climates can now occur only *outside* school settings. As practitioners, we should bring these theories into the classroom and use them in the following ways:

- as a framework for literacy teaching;

- to think about community, identity, race and language;

- to incorporate multimodality into literacy teaching and learning;

- to diversify linguistic repertoires;

- to account for forms and funds of knowledge, such as gardening, linguistic repertoires and home writing practices in our planning and teaching.

By supporting our students, we recognize the value of their ecological knowledge. We are also valuing their literacy, and fostering their identities in practice and across diasporas.

5

Literacy and identity: Who are the meaning makers?

Vignette: Identity mediation in online spaces

Amelia Wolfe, a high school English teacher in a small, suburban, regional New Jersey school district, believes in the importance of teaching traditional as well as twenty-first-century literacy skills. By the time spring rolled around each school year she was confident that her 10th Grade college preparation students were equipped with stronger writing skills than they began the year with, and that they were ready to tackle Psychoanalytic Character Analysis with a focus on the characters in *The Great Gatsby*. As always, after mini-lessons on Psychoanalytic Literary Theory and close readings and discussions of the text, Amelia assigned their final paper. The students were to choose a character from the novel and argue if the character was controlled by the Id, Ego, or Superego.

Amelia noticed that each year the students struggled not with the ability to write a traditional research paper, but with the ability to express complex analytical thoughts in written form. In response, she decided to add a twenty-first-century element to her traditional research paper assignment. Before beginning the actual writing process, Amelia had each student create a wiki where he or she completed specific tasks to help himself or herself understand which part of the psyche controlled his or her character's personality. For example, students were asked to answer questions such as: What people, things, or ideas control the choices your character makes? What is the biggest influence in your character's life? Can you create and explain a **symbol** for your character's identity? List quotations said by your character and decide which personality traits they reveal, and what

(Cont'd)

are the important relationships to people and things in your character's life? Each question or prompt was explored by each student in the form of:

- lists;

- charts;

- diagrams;

- images;

- audio clips, and/or

- short responses on his or her wiki page.

The students utilized multimodal forms and skills online that they would not be privy to if simply writing in a spiral-bound journal or notebook. Amelia was able to easily access and respond to each answer, often helping students to clarify their ideas and even suggesting other multimodal tools to help them express their thoughts. These tools ranged from programs like Garage Band, where they could compose their own music, to applications in Microsoft Office that allowed them to create charts and graphs. Moreover, classmates could view, comment, and offer suggestions about each other's work, and often gain more insight into their own character in the process.

The wiki allowed Amelia to monitor her students' brainstorming and idea development. In addition, the wiki also scaffolded the process of writing for students who were unable to simply and quickly take a topic, come up with an idea, and support those ideas on paper. After completing the wiki tasks, all students were in a much better and much more informed place to tackle the paper topic and to support their ideas. By using multimodal literacy skills and practices to support a traditional writing assignment, Amelia was able to show her students the value of both forms of representation and writing – especially issues dealing with identity and identity mediation.

Key themes in the chapter:

Identity-as-thing versus identity-in-practice

- New Literacy Studies, multimodality and identity

- Sedimented identity in texts

- Literacy, identity and place

- Identity, teaching and learning

- Critically framing identity

INTRODUCTION

Imagine a group of individuals whom you have recently taught or observed, and imagine their faces. Are they tired? Are they engaged? What are their interests and ruling passions? Equally, your feelings as a teacher are important. How do you feel? Do you find the class exhausting or tiring? Identity comes into teaching and learning, both for teachers and students.

- Who are your students and what kinds of emotions are they having as they learn?

These kinds of questions run through your mind when you spend time with a group of students. Such questions emerge from a desire, even a need, to understand the role of identity in learning. Identity and how identities function within classroom spaces and how they take up ideas is so much a part of teaching and learning. Within New Literacy Studies, identity, and identity mediation, is central to research and theory. In a collection Jennifer co-edited with Sandra Schamroth-Abrams (Schamroth-Abrams & Rowsell, 2011), they devoted the volume to examining identity as a part of the literacy process. In the introduction to the volume, they talk about a shift in new literacies research from looking at *identity-as-thing* to **identity-in-practice** (Leander, 2002: 198–199). For instance, an architect is an example of an identity in relation to a 'thing' (architect) rather than identity as nested in a place, or in doing certain actions. Rather than viewing identity (i.e., beliefs, dispositions, values, interests, background, etc.) as an object to analyze, identities are viewed in relation to actions and practices that are enacted to present identities in a particular light.

This insight constituted a theoretical shift from seeing identities as internally formed to seeing identities as *in practice*. This theoretical shift was marked by a spate of studies looking at the individual and community practices that help to shape one's identity. Through such research, literacy practices are perceived as a relationship between the actual practice (e.g., writing an email) and people's situated actions, behaviours, beliefs, values and discourses. By looking outside schooling, researchers can contrast how identities experience schooling spaces, and then contrast these identities with identities in spaces outside school. Expanding spaces to research identities in practice permitted researchers to recognize funds of knowledge that are not present in schooling and institutional settings (Moll et al., 1992).

- What kinds of knowledge do our students draw on in school?

This chapter considers how identities are formed and form in the sites that we inhabit, whether it is as a classroom teacher or as a Year 4 student or as a parent interacting with a child at home.

In the first edition of *Literacy and Education*, we noted that identity is potentially one of the most important ingredients of teaching and learning. The way that we express our identity is partly through language, but we also express our identity through our dress, our artifacts, our web presence, etc. In other words, we create our identity through our social practices. Our identity is supported in everyday social practice. Even in the five years since we wrote our first edition, there are more ways of mediating identity. For much of the time, language is used to construct an identity for ourselves within different speech communities that we enter and exit. For example, we can locate the place we live in through our accent.

At other times, visuals and interactive texts present an identity that we want to offer. Whenever we communicate, we are thinking about *who* is our audience, *where* and *what* is the context, and *how* do we behave in this setting? Communication regulates and mediates these factors. When we communicate, we are mediating our identity in practice. An unspoken truth about teaching and learning is that the more agency we give to students, the more they learn.

- How do we signal identities through modes other than language? In what forms do these identities appear?

Vignette: Theorizing literacy and identity from the location of the classroom

By Rob Simon

Literacy teacher researchers (e.g., Ballenger, 1999; Simon, 2005, 2009, 2012; Vasudevan, 2006; Christensen, 2009) have theorized the relationships of literacy and identity from and in classrooms, what Campano (2007) has described as sites of 'epistemic privilege'. Among other things, teacher researchers have explored the ways that adolescents' literacy practices are co-extensive with issues of identity, raising implications for literacy pedagogy.

I encouraged new teachers in my literacy curriculum and instruction course to regard their classrooms as sites of systematic and intentional inquiry (Cochran-Smith & Lytle, 2009), through ethnographic research projects. One literacy teacher, Aiden, encountered an 11th Grade student, Jared, who had experienced prior school failure, including being expelled in 8th Grade. Through an inquiry that explored adolescents' literacy practices at home and in school, Aiden discovered that counter to the institutional account of Jared's abilities, he was a motivated reader and writer. Jared announced the braided nature of literacy and identity in his life in conversation with Aiden, stating 'without comic books, there would be no me'.

Aiden recognized an opportunity to develop a more relational approach to teaching Jared. He encouraged Jared to develop his interest in comic books through arts-integrated inquiry projects exploring the work of Kafka and Marquez. Though their relationship was not without complication, Aiden was able to effectively advocate for Jared over time, helping him to navigate the challenges of the high school English curriculum, and eventually achieve admission to a prestigious arts college. This example illustrates how, as adolescents like Jared develop identities and abilities with particular forms of literacy, teachers can become more intentionally aware of their students' needs and interests. This may require countering autonomous conceptions of literacy (Street, 1995) through developing their own emic theories, and displacing institutional assumptions about students' abilities to know them – and teach them – differently.

When we consider identity, we also consider literacy. Literacy practices are infused with identity. Literacy is a culturally mediated and practice-infused activity that constantly pulls on the personality of the speaker, the writer, or the reader. Our ways of being, speaking, writing and reading are intimately bound up with the different discourse communities which in turn shape our identities further.

This chapter looks at how meaning makers embed parts of themselves in their literacy practices and how identities are played out as they cross sites.

We ask these questions:

- What happens to Dionne's Manga character when she takes her scrapbook from home to her classroom? (Chapter 2)

- How does Sabil's learning and connection to school shift after she constructs and maintains a garden at her school? (Chapter 4)

- What happens when Francene Planas' 5th Grade class makes a book out of student self-portraits and they actually see themselves in their learning? (This chapter)

What happens is that identities are invited into classroom spaces. This process, then, closes a gap between school and home.

Vignette: 'Our Amazing Pictures' – an interdisciplinary 5th Grade ELL literacy project in Paraguay

By Francene Planas

I am a photographer and educator with over 20 years' experience teaching elementary-level ELL students writing in schools in New York City, Mexico and Paraguay. My methodology is to create books combining children's photographs and drawings with their writing. The participants come with differing needs and backgrounds, some non-English speaking, and of every ability level from special education to gifted. These books of young learners' visions and thoughts use themes from their lives, ethnic heritages, communities, and classroom curricula. By focusing on the parallels between visual and written literacy, these projects provide new ways for ELL learners to explore critical thinking while developing multi-language writing enrichment. Those with difficulty verbalizing are given the chance to first visualize their ideas, preparing them for multilingual creative writing acquisition. Others have opportunities to develop what they have achieved in the written medium by expressing ideas pictorially. Furthermore, each student learns the ways pictures and words enhance one another through sequencing and editing the individual works into a unified expression of a book.

I believe photography is a powerful medium of expression and teaching tool because it is documentary, editorial, and emotive in nature. It is a universal communicator that children respond to easily, teaching them to observe their environment in new ways while augmenting linguistic growth. Furthermore, designing and constructing a book is mentally similar to composing a written essay. Contributing to the book's theme, design, content and title raises students' self-esteem and produces confidence as well as enthusiasm for the writing process.

With an ELL 5th Grade class in Paraguay, I created a ten-week self-portrait project, which became a book that the students entitled 'Our Amazing Pictures'. We began by looking at photography books of portraits from different cultures and eras. We went to see a museum photography exhibit about Brazilians. While observing these pictures, students discussed how people dress and look differently. I suggested that for the next class students bring or wear an object that showed something special about themselves for their portrait.

In the next session, each pupil chose a pose and I photographed him or her. After the pictures were taken, students selected their favourite portrait from the series for the book. I worked with each child as they reflected and verbalized in English on their image. The students shared their thoughts, relationships and feelings, which were not visible in the portraits, with the rest of the class. Afterwards students began writing their comments in English. We combined the writing and photograph on a single page for

Figure 5.1   Alberto

each participant and sequenced the book in alphabetical order by first name. The students named their book, and we combined it with a photograph of everyone's hands for the cover. They commented 'We like having a book with all our friends in it'. We made 60 bound, hard covers, and photocopied books. Every student received a copy as well as the school library, principal and teachers. Parents requested more copies to give to relatives. The school librarian told me it was one of the most read books, everyone in the school enjoyed reading it. The principal got funds to individually frame each page for a school lobby exhibit. The 5th Grade students were very proud and wanted to write more books together.

Identity breathes life into literacy in so many ways. It could be a teenager adding photographs of an event on to his or her *Facebook* page. It could be a mother who had recently arrived in Toronto from Pakistan displaying family photos on her mantelpiece. It could be a child purchasing a scarf for her penguin within the virtual world of Club Penguin. Or, it could be a teacher putting students' names on their cubbies at the beginning of the school year. Harnessing literacy teaching to identity is so important, and is often so undermined in policy and pedagogy.

Think about the process of going to school. Often a student has to wear different clothes (uniform) and operate within a different timescale (the school day) as well as in specific spaces. The spaces that are constructed for learning are different from the spaces at home. In a recent study, Kate asked young children to research reading in their school. They found that the children preferred to read on beds, on comfortable cushions, or to their pets or siblings. These kinds of spaces are less available in school settings.

• What and where are the spaces where you like to read?

This study helped us see the way schooling positions students' identities over other identities, perhaps more eclectic identities. It happens far too frequently that students acquire an identity within a classroom, for instance a child who is unable to read or to write. Meanwhile, at home or in mosque, that same child draws elaborate pictures with accompanying oral tales or they can recite by rote large segments of the Quran. These literate moments, and they are indeed literate moments, are clear evidence of literacy practices, but there is a mismatch between inside and outside school identities. These two discursive identities are different. A **discursive identity** is one that is constructed within discourse, within speaking, within designing language. There can be such a disparity between school spaces and homes and communities. In Chapter 3, the expression 'third space' was used to describe the meeting point between home and school. This third space can be filled with students' identities – such as Amelia Wolfe's secondary classroom or Francene Planas' Grade 5 ELL classroom. Both of these contexts offered students a third space where out-of-school literacies were allowed into the classroom.

Theory Box: Cultural-historical activity theory and identity

Cultural-historical activity theory (CHAT) suggests that a shared social context is **dialogic** and firmly rooted in the context being studied (Gutiérrez & Stone, 2000; Wells & Claxton, 2002). CHAT is a helpful concept to think about in relation to literacy and identity. CHAT offers a useful lens for considering multimodal literacy practices as we extend conceptions of context to the 'third space', a virtual reality that blurs modes of communication, including oral language, printed text, fixed and moving images, and widening opportunities for audience involvement (Gutiérrez, 2008). Within CHAT, teachers and students are positioned within multiple economic, intellectual, social and spatial systems that situate these agents' construction of knowledge. CHAT takes up the notion of identity and shared context as informing learning. See Figure 5.2 – CHAT in practice.

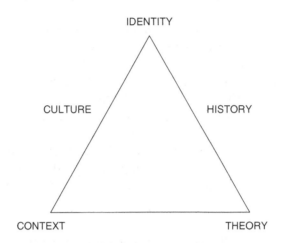

Figure 5.2   Literacy and identity

CHAT enables us to understand the way in which different identities work in a shared site, such as an after-school club or a neighbourhood. The theory helps us see how identities are both similar and shared. For example, in a particular district in Princeton, USA, two neighbours may share the same heritage (Hispanic) but have very different economic trajectories, one being an academic and the other working as a house cleaner for a living. Yet both can trace their ancestry back to similar roots.

CHAT helps us trace the arc of students' identities through what they do and how they position themselves within these trajectories.

STUDIES OF LITERACY AND IDENTITY

Our identities are formed, bound up in the way in which we speak and act. Writing and literacy are social and cultural processes that relate to our cultural identity. The way that we see the world is a part of our identity. Identity is the filter through which we present ourselves to the world. Literacy practices at home and at school link with students' evolving sense of themselves as cultural agents.

- How can teachers respond to this challenge?

When we teach language, there may be a clash between our students' identities and the curriculum. It is often through our identity that these differences emerge. When students interact with language, their identity infuses that language. When students grow up in homes and communities, they carry with them the shared cultural spaces, the church, the movies and the habits that their homes and communities engage with.

Many studies have examined how identity informs literacy practices. Donna Alvermann continues to explore how adolescents engage in multiple, complex practices in order to explore identities (Alvermann, 2002). Elizabeth Moje in her research has found that music and rap contributed to literacy practices that young people bring into classrooms (Moje et al., 2004). Luke and Carrington have also looked at young children and their 'glocalized' literacy practices, which need to be acknowledged in classroom settings (Luke & Carrington, 2002). Students have ideas and experiences that they bring with them from other places. These are inscribed into their literacy practices and travel with them.

 Points of Reflection: Capturing identity

Imagine that you had to create a portrait of your identity – your background, your idiosyncrasies, your values, your beliefs, your teaching philosophy. What would it look like? Plan a portrait, which can be in a digital forum or a scrapbook or even a backpack filled with artifacts of self. Reflect on these questions as you plan and assemble materials:

- What artifact reflects my values and beliefs?
- What text or image reflects my background?
- How would you describe yourself to someone?
- What is your philosophy of learning?
- How would you plan a lesson shaped on this philosophy?
- Describe how you would mediate your identity as you cross from one context to the next (e.g., from home to school).

Now, develop a portrait using these questions to frame its development.

SPACE AND IDENTITY

Identity pulls on place in a way that we did not truly appreciate in the first edition of *Literacy and Education*, before we conducted ecological work.

Ecological work captures the interdependence that happens within communities when people rely on resources in their immediate environment for everyday practice.

Conducting ecological work, going on neighbourhood walk-arounds and speaking with community members, consolidates a deeper understanding of space and place. Researchers have investigated the relationship between space, time and identity for some time. Researchers such as Barbara Comber and Helen Nixon have conducted research in Australia looking at the role of space and place in relation to children's meaning-making. In their work together, Comber and Nixon have brought together a focus on literacy and place to study students in their changing physical and semiotic environments, particularly in areas with urban regeneration (Nixon & Comber, 2006; Comber et al. 2007). Nixon and Comber have also collaborated with teachers to undertake inquiries into the integration of place studies in schools located in communities living with land degeneration and severe drought in towns and settlements (Nixon, 2007). This research has focused on the school as a site for learning which carries the potential to help students engage in real-world place studies, for example, mapping the neighbourhood or using *Google Maps* to engage with place.

 Activity

Space, Place and Identity

Begin a unit on space and place by locating your school in *Google Earth* on an interactive white board or on a screen during a lesson. Then move through these ideas:

As a follow-up, ask students to create an artifactual map of their community. That is, locate key and meaningful landmarks in their communities and add in connected stories (perhaps through vectors that look like hypertext) about the artifacts.

For the next lesson, have students walk around the school, talking about the community and key landmarks around the school grounds.

Then ask a community member to speak with the class about their community and perhaps the history of the community.

Finally, as a culminating activity, ask students to work with a partner to complete a scavenger hunt around the school to find key artifacts with post-it notes or cue cards detailing their history and importance. Have students draw a map of their route during the scavenger hunt. To make the activity more digital, ask students to use tools such as Mapping for Everyone or *Google Earth*.

Time and space are important markers on identity. Timescales structure the way we conceive ourselves, as born in relation to a set of intergenerational experiences and practices. The space we inhabit structures who we are. If we live in a neighbourhood where our family live, we can locate our intergenerational selves within the households that live nearby. This provides a settled account of our identities in practice. Migration can create a hole in these experiences that takes its toll. Accounting for these identities is important when considering literacy in the classroom.

Vignette: The story of the suitcase

I (Kate) interviewed a family whose grandparents had migrated from Pakistan to the UK in the 1950s to make a new life. In an interview with Roxana, she described her father's suitcase, and all the labels it carried:

Kate: And you also talked about an old suitcase?

Roxana: Yes, mum's, I do believe she has still got it. I will ask her. I remember very vividly as a child this brown leather suitcase with all these labels on it. I assume they had labels at that time – they weren't the kind you could take off – and mum saying dad had used it for several years, and this is all the places he had gone to – I think she's got it somewhere. (Interview, RK, Rotherham, South Yorkshire, UK September 19, 2006)

Figure 5.3   Suitcase, by Zahir Rafiq

What was interesting about the suitcase was that the family never actually found the original. Instead, as part of the project, an artist, Zahir Rafiq, created a new version, pictured in Figure 5.3. What this image did was pull on the identities of the family, who travelled between continents, from Pakistan to New York, Rotherham and then to Kuwait and Indochina, over the years.

Vignette: Videoing chapatti-making as home digital literacy practice

By Parven Akhter

The family involved in this case study were second and third-generation British-Pakistani. I met them during my previous work as a community development practitioner. The first generation of this family (the grandfather) came from Pakistan in the 1960s and worked in a cotton mill in London. The daughter is the second generation of the family and one of her children, Amina, is third generation and is a 10-year-old Year 5 student at primary school. The mother used to work in the voluntary sector within the community and has four children: three girls aged 12, 10 and 1, and a 3-year-old boy. The study was located in the family kitchen where the mother was making chapattis. Amina expressed her interest in and curiosity about the process involved in making chapattis. A home video was taken by Amina while her mother was making chapattis. The mother's activities involved in making chapattis were imitated by Amina. The food-making (chapatti) practice was captured as part of their everyday family life routines. The child mentioned that she herself had chosen to video chapatti-making. She said that she ate it almost every day and liked to see how it was made.

The video was taken by Amina on April 1, 2010 at 7pm. In the video Amina said:

> OK, this is how we make chapatti. It's really good and my mum is making it. First you roll it like that and then you squiggle it, squiggle it, quite a lot of times. Then you put some of this. [The mother remarked 'It's dry flour'.] OK, put some dry flour on it and then when you do this, you start rolling it with this. [The mother said, 'It's a rolling pin'.] (See Figure 5.4)

The video demonstrated that Amina was adopting a multi-tasking approach which involved both verbal and non-verbal communication with her mother while simultaneously operating the video camera in order to focus on and capture the target points involved in the food-making process. These target points included activities relating to the frying pan, the gas cooker, the dough making – using flour, salt and

(Cont'd)

Figure 5.4   Chapatti-making (1)

water, the rolling pin and griddle, etc. I observed from the video that the child was recording the chapatti-making event very confidently and capably. I noted the use of the video camera was a way of developing hand–eye co-ordination and also showed that demonstration activities can develop presentation skills.

> After you do this, you put it on the frying pan, whenever you put it on and do that (one after another side is put on the hot pan). We will show you later on. This is dry flour. This is *roti* (bread). [The mother made the correction 'That is dough'.] That is made of flour, salt and water. We can see that mum is making it bigger and bigger. And then you start [to] pattern it. Then one hand to another, then it will be much bigger. Then you put it on the frying pan and gas fire on it. Then put your hand on it and twist it gently round and round one side to [the] other side. Then it will make it warmer and warmer one side to other. Then you put this thing (rolling pin) on it and move that frying pan on the side and then you start moving it one

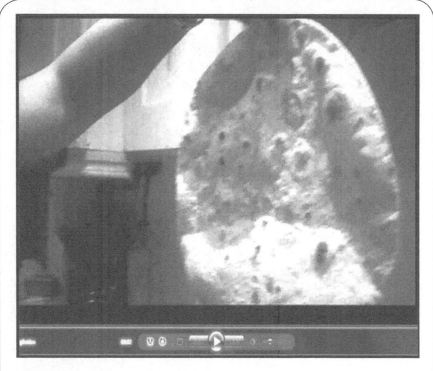

Figure 5.5   Chapatti-making (2)

side then other side. You see it gets bigger and bigger. When you put it down in the fire it gets bigger, and then it's cooked chapatti. (See Figure 5.5)

I also observed that the mother's purpose was two-fold in that she wanted not only to demonstrate, but also educate her daughter about making chapattis and about some of the transnational kitchen objects that appear in the video. These are cooking objects in the kitchen such as the rolling pin (*bolon*), frying pan (*taoya*), and the griddle traditionally designed for South Asian cooking. The concept of this practice is generative learning, passing from generation to generation. I found that it would be useful to theorize the practices of this chapatti (food)-making as cultural resources which contribute to the original concept of 'funds of knowledge' (Moll et al., 1992) and then further developed by Gonzalez, Moll and Amanti (2005).

The mother's comment on the video recording about her daughter:

She always likes something to do with technology. She made a PowerPoint presentation by using her auntie's wedding pictures and presented it in her school using a computer. She enjoyed doing this

(Cont'd)

chapatti video while I was making it. It is very good. Now she knows how to make it. She played this in the computer and watched it with her sister. It is our culture that girls (9 to 11years) are expected to learn cooking at primary school level. A few days ago, the staff from my son's nursery asked me to provide some Asian food-making recipes. They have lots of Asian kids in their nursery and they want to cook some Asian food. She mentioned that this is a good idea to video while cooking and produce a CD rather than providing written recipes.

The mother's comments about her daughter using the computer to watch the video with her sister showed that the girl was able to use information in digital format which was presented as instructions on the screen in order to present the video via a computer. The mother's comments 'It is our culture that girls (9 to 11years) are expected to learn cooking at primary school level' indicates this cultural importance. I also identified how cultural practices situated in the home relate to digital literacy practices and the way in which children's learning is constructed through watching videos. This learning involves the use of multiple modes of human interaction when they learned how to make chapattis.

In this vignette, we see how culture and identity infuse multimodal text-making. The process of meaning-making is shaped by intergenerational interaction and captured within the camera. Here, identities and cultures are used to shape home digital literacy practices.

The link between identities and texts is often embedded in a series of moments and arcs in time. Timescales contribute to identities as generations shape and develop the stories we hear in the home. Identities are entangled with time and space. This is an insight we have brought to the second edition of *Literacy and Education*.

Theory Box: Catherine Compton-Lilly on how time and space play key roles in positioning identity

Compton-Lilly (2007, 2010) examines closely case studies of African-American youth and their ten-year journeys through schooling in the Rochester area. In her work, Compton-Lilly theorizes how time and space play roles in the forging of identities. For example, a 'good reader' in 1st Grade can become a different person over time, as the experience of schooling can create deficit models of identity that stop students seeing themselves as positive, literate identities within school. This means that teachers need to open up literacy experiences for their students that honour their identities. Intersecting with literacy learning, Compton-Lilly argues that teachers can use media and cultural resources to create learning experiences that are responsive to individual students. Compton-Lilly opens our eyes to ways in which educators have to account for race and culture in their teaching, and she illustrates strongly in her work the inextricable tie between literacy and identity over time and across space.

HOW CAN STUDENTS' IDENTITIES BE EXPLORED IN CLASSROOMS?

There are ways within the classroom to mediate identity with curriculum. There can be meeting spaces where a student's own identity in practice can be opened up and explored. One way is to identify a student's language needs based on what they know and what they have experienced. If we work within Moje's third space, we focus on how identities are made within, through and against available representations (Moje et al., 2004). You can encourage students to keep a reading log; if they are young, parents can be involved in the activity that charts every literacy event (at home and at school) they embark on.

- Think of some literacy practices that pull on identities. For example, *Facebook*, blogs, *Twitter*, or writing a note to a friend. What kinds of practices can you identify with your students?

As literacy teachers, we have to remember that children are limited to public spaces that are constructed for them and, importantly, these spaces operate on the basis that children have something *to do* within them. There are not many opportunities within classroom spaces to manifest or to celebrate student identities. Francene Planas celebrated student identities by making a book out of student self-portraits. Keeping a log of students' experiences and artifacts can be transferred to classroom walls and can become a subject for discussion about literacy practices in everyday life. Students can take disposable cameras home to record the reading activity that goes on in the home – on a computer, or reading the television guides and football scores.

By acknowledging your students' literacy practices, you are acknowledging their identities. These identities will then become more visible in the classroom. The space of the classroom and the walls and the physical environment can support your students' identities in practice. They can be encouraged to bring in from outside the classroom the identity markers they feel close to. For example, in a family literacy class, a Turkish child drew flags of Turkey, as identity markers. A project on Paul Klee led to young children drawing the flats they lived in, in the style of Klee. A discussion ensued about the geographies of space in the city.

A key element of this work recognizes that identities can be expressed in artifacts, which can then cross sites. In the case of Winston's admission letter to Rutgers University (see Chapter 1), it is a meaningful artifact because it combines his identities (of his Haitian roots along with his American life, his divided loyalties, his aspirations for himself and his country of origin) and serves as an identity artifact. Winston also mediates his identity through *Facebook* and an online presence, where he can cross cultures and contexts through virtual spaces.

- What happens to literacy practices when they cross sites?

Theory Box: Guy Merchant on identity mediation in digital worlds

For some time now, Guy Merchant has researched and written about the intersection of digital literacy and identity. Digital literacy refers to the 'study of written or symbolic representation that is mediated by new technology' (Merchant, 2007: 121). Digital spaces have become a leading forum for identity mediation because they allow individuals to be creative with who they are in virtual worlds (i.e., they are not constrained by their situations, their appearances, etc.). Having freedom and licence to create identities online and offline has made identity mediation more nuanced. According to Merchant, digital literacy has resulted in such shifts in composition as:

1 Text is no longer fixed, but fluid. Limitations of text in book form or page form are no longer the case.

2 There is more of an intertextual nature to compositions that often allows for more identity investment.

3 Texts are easily reformatted, revised, updated, accessed and supplemented.

4 Texts are, or can be, collaborative. With multiple voices of contributions, the roles of the reader and the writer become linked and overlapping.

5 The pathways of reading and writing are frequently non-linear.

6 Texts are multimodal with a rich interplay of modalities.

7 Communicative space is often shared and crosses geographical boundaries (local and global).

---

8 'Synchronous engagement increases' (2007: 122).

9 Personal boundaries blur – professional, recreational, public, private, serious and trivial become blurred within online spaces.

Through his work, Merchant has allowed researchers to recognize that individuals anchor identities online that are often different from their offline identities, and it is important to acknowledge and respect the difference.

Digitized artifacts, such as blogs, wikis, social networking sites, can therefore be infused with identity. It can be an authentic picture of your identity, or you can experiment with alternative realities. For example, many games involve the construction of an **avatar**, an imaginary computer-generated icon which travels as the person through the game. The player constructs an avatar in a game which then is used as an expression of identity. Children who play avatar games such as Wii or Club Penguin infuse their avatars with their own identity in practice (Pahl, 2005). Children can then slip in and out of these identities when playing games.

- Would you create an avatar like you or would you create an alternative identity?

Vignette: Getting hyper(link)ed about poetry

By Anne Peel

A spontaneous and audible groan erupted from Anne Peel's 10th Grade English class when she announced the beginning of a three-week poetry unit.

'I don't get poetry. It doesn't make any sense.'

'Are you gonna make us write poems? We have to do this every year and I just can't write poetry.'

'Are we gonna study the kind that don't rhyme? I just can't get into poems that don't rhyme.'

Resistance, hostility, confusion: the students' reactions indicate that their prior studies of poetry had conditioned them to fear it. In order to tap into the class' digital, multimodal literacies, and thereby make the poems more accessible, Anne decided to conduct some of the poetry lessons on the

(Cont'd)

class wiki which she had set up using wikispaces.org. The digital affordances of the wiki, such as hyperlinks and discussion boards, allowed the class to establish their own interpretative context through a social network. Within this context, each poem became a conduit for meaning-making rather than an obstacle to comprehension, a resource rather than a riddle.

The first poem the class studied was 'Somewhere I Have Never Travelled', by e. e. cummings, a poem full of the kinds of non-rhyming, figurative obscurities that had proved so intimidating. During the lesson, the students logged on to the site, and used the navigation bar to find a digital copy of the poem. Anne had created hyperlinks from particular words, phrases and lines in the poem that led to interpretative questions about that portion of the text. The students chose any link that interested them, and were then instructed to use the discussion board on that page to answer the question or respond to a prior comment.

The questions targeted different types of analysis and offered different amounts of overt instructional support. For example, the hyperlink of the first line, 'Somewhere I have never travelled', led to the question 'Where is the place that the poet has not travelled? In what way is this a good metaphor for a new relationship?' The question scaffolds the students' learning by offering a model of interpretation. Other questions, however, require the reader to analyze the poet's language by injecting it with their own identities. For example, the phrase, 'the voice of your eyes is deeper than all roses' leads to the question 'What figure of speech is being used here? Is there anyone you have this feeling about, that you can hear the voice of their eyes?'

When the poems for the unit of study were relocated to the wiki space, they were transformed from print-based, largely monomodal texts that adhered to the logic of the page, to interactive, multimodal texts that adhered to the logic of the screen; they were repositioned as conduits for socially-situated meaning construction rather than embodiments of an author's intended truth. This transformation not only encouraged students to engage in meaning-making, but also redistributed the privileged status of the text by visually situating the **reader's response** within the digitally layered textual space. Students travelled along their own individual reading paths through the poem in an active, almost physical way as they clicked on links, typed in comments, and scrolled through discussions.

By the end of the unit, the students were thrilled to post their own original work on to the wiki and create hyperlinked questions from the words and phrases they selected from their poems. The 10th Graders read their peers' work, dived into their questions, and offered feedback and interpretation, weaving together their roles as reader and writer in a wonderfully tangled matrix of deeply engaged literacy practices. Hostility and fear became enthusiasm and delight as the 10th Graders all built their own route to 'get into' poetry.

IDENTITIES-IN-PRACTICE: WHAT CHILDREN BRING TO THEIR TEXTS

In Chapters 2 and 3, we talked about how texts carry the interest of the sign-maker which relates strongly to the theme of literacy and identity. To conceptualize this idea, Kate and I have developed a theory of sedimented identities in texts.

Theory Box: Kate Pahl and Jennifer Rowsell on sedimented identities in texts

A Turkish child, Fatih, drew a picture of a chicken on a piece of paper. This drawing represented the experience he has, aged 5-years old, of chasing the chickens on his grandparents' farm in Turkey. Over time, Fatih became obsessed with birds and his drawings reflected this identity. Fatih's drawings were textual artifacts that constituted traces of social practice. The experience of chasing the chickens turned into a drawing.

Viewing artifacts as tracers of identity led Kate and I to develop a theory of sedimented identity in texts. The theorizing grew out of a marriage of New Literacy Studies, multimodality, and Bourdieu's notion of habitus (Bourdieu, 1990), that is, a combination of literacy as social practice, the visual through multimodality and the way life is lived, the habitus.

New Literacy Studies signalled a social turn in literacy when literacy was and is viewed as a set of practices that are shaped by context. Multimodality signalled a semiotic turn in literacy when literacy was viewed as semiotic not solely as a linguistic system. Bourdieu (1990) defined habitus as ways of being, doing and acting in the world across generations. In *Artifactual Literacies*, Kate and I draw further on habitus as the everyday, lived experiences and unfolding of dispositions of meaning makers (Pahl & Rowsell, 2010). Sedimented identities in texts merge all three areas together (NLS, multimodality and Bourdieu) as a theorizing of the way in which texts are materially constructed by identities in practice. In an article that describes the process, we claim that:

> The theory rests on a contemplation of the moment of production – the context, the producer with his or her set of dispositions, the text and what it points to, and how it reflects the context in which it was made. (Rowsell & Pahl, 2007: 394)

The notion of sedimented identities informs this book because the kind of sedimenting of context, of producer subjectivities, of global and local ideologies takes place when students describe the moments of their production.

(Cont'd)

Sedimented identity excavates how texts get their meaning and form, and also how texts signal material and immaterial worlds.

It is then possible to view children's texts as a serious attempt to create meanings from experiences over time and to represent those meanings anew. Many of these texts are drawn or modelled; these also matter to the meaning makers who created them.

Children are in the process of being and then becoming. They are in process (Uprichard, 2008). Children are becoming – children are about to be grown up or a teenager. Children care about their siblings and what their siblings think. There is a forwards and backwards. Identities are networked in different ways through media and music. Hubs are outside and inside school.

 Activity

Timeline of Sedimented Identities in Texts

Timelines can be a productive way of illustrating not only how we sediment identity into texts, but also how our production of texts shifts over time.

To have students actively use the notion of sedimented identities in texts, create your own timeline of texts that embed parts of yourself – perhaps a childhood artifact, an artifact that reflects your youth, a lesson plan or adult artifact – so that you model for students how you have actively embedded your own identity into texts.

Then have students create a timeline on a blank piece of paper that represents texts of self, as in the figure below.

←↓-------------------------------↓-------------------------------↓------------------→

Childhood drawing   School assignment or   Picture as an adult
                           creative writing

Then, have students work in small groups to present their timelines. These timelines can be used to create plans for a digital story about a student's life, or to plan a storyboard for a film. Creating formats for the representation of identities is generative of future literacy work. It is then possible to construct timelines that represent particular facets of the self (e.g., in relation to favourite artifacts such as songs or television programmes or toys) that can show developing trajectories and experiences.

When we consider our students, their experience is always represented in discourse. They have different identities for different communities they exist within. A child may speak a home language at home, and English at school. These complex identities, which are connected to different sites, are part of who our students are. They may also encounter different '**figured worlds**' through their out-of-school activities, including virtual worlds, the worlds of popular culture and fantasy.

Theory Box: Dorothy Holland on identities in figured worlds

Dorothy Holland argues that 'People tell others who they are, but even more importantly, they tell themselves and then try to act as though they are who they say they are' (Holland et al., 2001: 3). Holland and colleagues argued that people *create* identities. They argue that identity is a concept that works to connect the intimate or personal world with the wider world of social relations. Identities are located in 'figured worlds', which are spaces where social encounters are experienced and realized. They are collective, 'as if' realms that can be experienced in narrative or through artifacts, which open up figured worlds. Holland's theory of identity rests on identities-in-practice being bound up with figured worlds. Identities are part of the accumulation of history; they are 'history in person' (Holland et al., 2001; Holland & Lave, 2001).

For example, your students might have a figured world at home that is World of Warcraft, which is a space of practice and is an entire 'as if realm'. Within this world, your student might have an avatar and a script which is important. Or a student might play on Club Penguin and have a particular character which means a lot to him or her. These figured worlds provide scripts for students to draw on and develop. In the classroom, these scripts can become storyboards for a film or sources for a piece of narrative text they can turn into stories.

- What adjective describes a figured world? For example, what is 'home' and 'work' for you?

CONCLUSION

We should try to locate teaching and learning within the identities our students bring to our classrooms. These identities are networked, and cross local and global spaces. They relate to local hubs for literacy, such as libraries, and friendships within those spaces, as well as friendships which stretch half way across the globe, through *Facebook*. Understanding these networked identities is a challenge for our practice in the class-room. They reveal literacy practices that are distributed, participatory and in practice.

Luke and Carrington argue that we need to fuse the local literacy prac-tices with which our students engage with the global literacies they bring through the Internet, into a new 'glocalized' literacy that can be used within curricula settings (Luke & Carrington, 2002). This form of literacy is the local infused with the global, and the global infused with the local. Each speaks to each other and each has a relationship to each other. Working out what these practices can do for us in our lives is part of the job of schooling.

Schools can provide 'third spaces' which can enable students' identities to be recognized. This can bring in community interests, the ways in which the community works. Students' use of local community resources can be brought into the school. In the UK, community schools acknowl-edge the diverse communities they serve (Nixon, Allan & Mannion, 2001). Family literacy classes can become spaces where families can bring cultural identities, family narratives and children's experience can be recognized and built upon in spaces which are neither classrooms nor homes, but in-between spaces. Digital literacies can be drawn upon to create shared classroom spaces such as blogs, wikis and Prezis. Types of text can be brainstormed within the classroom. Identities can be evoked in these discussions. Research carried out by children and families can inform curricular choices that schools can make about what they teach and how. Researching literacy practices in the community (as described in Chapter 3) can enrich this process.

Much of what our students do is creative in an everyday sense. The role of creativity in literacy learning is hinged to identities and the way in which we learn is extended through creativity in learning. This can be creative in visual or linguistic modes. Students can be stretched in their learning as they use expressive language to write rap poems, develop art and poetry on blogs and wikis, design new presentations on a Prezi and learn to love language. In so doing, they use new vocabulary to develop new identities, as successful learners. Language becomes a tool for iden-tity and for developing new identities.

Classrooms are spaces that can be infused with our students' identities. This is a challenge, to move the focus from the centre of the room to the circle around the room. Identities play a foundational role in our students' literacy development. When we speak, we enact our identity. As children come to write, the host of experiences that they have had since birth are brought to bear on literacy practices. By recognizing and honouring that experience, we are bringing our students' identities into the classrooms and, like Winston's admission's letter, letting them flourish.

To think about ...

Challenging our Notions and Understandings of Text

By Cheryl A. McLean

As a secondary school English teacher, and now as an academic and professor of literacy education, my approach to teaching has always been about positionality combined with a critical pedagogy approach with an expanded view of what literacy is in the twenty-first-century. What this means for my teaching is that I try to challenge students to critically frame language against issues of culture and identity.

It is not uncommon to have the pre-service teachers with whom I work, unpack their conceptions of what is 'text', and I challenge them to think about how their notions of text inform what they choose to do in the classroom – the texts they use, the choices they make, and the texts and literacy practices they value in the classroom. One such teachable moment arose in a discussion of 'must read' texts. I asked the teachers to brainstorm a list of texts that they considered their top ten 'must reads' for their adolescent students.

The Scenario: What would be your top ten texts that you believe all adolescent students should read? As the teachers each made their way up to the board to add their texts to the ever-expanding list, there was a noticeable trend: the texts that these beginning teachers had chosen for their students could all be categorized as the 'canon' and 'traditional' texts.

The Challenge: I then raised some probing questions: How many of these texts are (1) magazines, (2) graphic novels/comic, (3) about and/or written by persons of colour, (4) about and/or written by women, (5) about and/or written by persons who identify as gay, lesbian or transgender, (6) set in contexts outside the USA, (7) digital, zines, fansites/fanfiction, blogs or social networking sites ...

The Reflection: My questions had given them pause for thought. I could see mixed reactions, ranging from surprise to thoughtfulness, as they each took notice of the fact that they found themselves often unable to answer affirmatively to some of the probing questions. I invited the group to write their reflections – they could use their notebooks or post their entry on their blogs in the class website. Then we shared the reflections and talked about what they were seeing; what thoughts the questions provoked;

(Cont'd)

what their choices said about their values, beliefs and practices. During the discussion, Dwight ventured .... *'You know, I hadn't ever thought of texts and the canon in that way. To be honest, when you put it this way, I hate to think of how many students I'm failing if I continue to teach only what I've been taught, and how I've been taught.'*

The Re-visioning: Kim blogged, *'I'd always thought of myself as a progressive teacher – as someone who knows her stuff. But, this activity made me really think about the values I bring to the classroom and how this might really prevent me from reaching many of my students.'*

One year later, Joanne shared, *'I've been rethinking "what is text?". And, now, I'm working with my department to begin to revise the curriculum. We're trying to provide more diversity. As for me? I've been bringing in more real-world texts in my classes, and I'm seeing students respond in a whole new way.'*

I would say that, for these teachers, the critical work has begun.

Navigating new literacies for new times: Shaping curriculum and pedagogy

---

Vignette: Opening new doors to literacy

By Rahat Naqvi

As part of my research in the area of multilingualism, I asked my pre-service teachers to use dual-language books in their field placements in elementary schools. During their practicum, they were asked to critically reflect on their pedagogy and the relevance of the dual-language books as a resource to advance early literacy learning for multilingual/multicultural learners.

Sara, an elementary pre-service teacher, was placed in a Grade 5 classroom. Sara was a child of immigrant parents and in her initial years in Canada was considered to be an English as a second language (ELL) learner. Her own experiences as a student from a different culture gave her an empathetic edge when it came to relating to students in her classroom who were also sharing in the immigrant experience. Sara had a strong desire to accommodate the ELL students in her classroom by enriching their lives with memorable and affirmative learning experiences and encouraging them to approach their new school and culture in a positive, confident manner, while at the same time acknowledging their native language and culture.

For her practicum, Sara was placed in a linguistically rich and culturally diverse school in northeast Calgary. Her classroom consisted of a group of Grade 5 students, the majority of whom were students whose first

(Cont'd)

---

language was not English. During the course of her practicum, she introduced the idea of reading dual-language books in the classroom. As many of her students spoke Punjabi and Urdu, she was certain there would not be a shortage of volunteers who would be willing to participate in a dual-language reading. In fact, Jamal, one of the Urdu-speaking students and a newly arrived immigrant from Pakistan, could hardly contain his excitement when he approached her to ask if he would be allowed to read the first dual-language story with her. He excitedly told Sara that he knew how to read and write in Urdu. He took the book home with him to practise reading with his parents. After a week, Jamal read to his fellow classmates with pride and they listened intently. As he read, it became evident that there were several students who understood Urdu. Even though there were those who did not, the reading provoked many interesting questions about the language, script and intonation. Shortly after this first dual-language reading, ten students in the classroom approached Sara and asked if they, too, could participate through reading in their native language. Although many of the students were only able to read a few words, all were very enthusiastic to take home books to practise with their parents.

⊙━ Key themes in the chapter:

- Possible literacy worlds for our students
- Researching literacy practices with teachers, students and parents
- Transforming literacy practices in classroom settings drawing on this research
- Curriculum (i.e., what is taught, often inscribed in documents and disseminated and formed at national level)
- Pedagogy (i.e., the way in which the curriculum is interpreted and taught and the assumptions behind that teaching that guide and shape teachers' practices)

INTRODUCTION

Imagine a classroom that speaks to the needs and interests of *all* students. This classroom works interchangeably in two and three dimensions, in print and in virtual worlds. Students access online and offline literacies with ease. This is a classroom that builds on situated research by students and teachers into home literacy practices to inform school literacy practices and extends and bridges home and school literacy practices. This classroom engages meaning makers and opens itself out to communities. It is a classroom at the interface of teacher identity and student identity *and* at practice/pedagogy and curriculum. It is a hub for literacy in the community. It is the kind of classroom we want to create for our students.

- What possible worlds can our students inhabit? What will the classroom of tomorrow look like?

In the classroom of tomorrow, literacy instruction will involve tasks that include problem-solving, research and analysis, and will engage with multiple literacy practices using print and visual, electronic, face-to-face media in combinations that are occurring in new, civic, media and workplace contexts.

INGREDIENTS OF THE NEW CLASSROOM

- Discussion and debate will form a fundamental part of this process, and the building of new concepts will link with the identities and motivations of students in contemporary contexts.

- Students are given the opportunity to develop critical literacy skills, involving second-guessing, criticizing, and arguing with a range of texts, and understanding their sources, production and power relations.

- The discussion would also involve a focus on objects where the values and concepts of the world would be interrogated in relation to artifacts (objects, realia) in this work and use them to interrogate and write about home and community contexts.

- Students would engage in collaborative work that involves collaborative reading, writing and decision-making in literacy events and practices within and across learning communities. This work will take place online and offline.

- Research would be conducted in home and community settings. Students and teachers would decide on research topics, carry out research studies, analyze the data and write the data up for policy-makers to read. Their findings would aid literacy development.

- Students would engage in **intercultural communication** that involves negotiating and solving problems across cultures and languages, and understanding the residual and emergent traditions within different cultures. As the vignette opening to this chapter shows, multilingual teaching and learning works.

- Reasons to write are clear in classrooms. Future classrooms involve both global and local analyses that incorporate understanding the diversity of the funds of knowledge that students bring to the classroom. Learning is situated and literacy has a purpose.

- Identities are harnessed to literacy activities in the classroom. A wide range of texts is available to students in future classrooms, including popular cultural texts. Students access academic language through their own literacy practices and then transform these vernacular practices into academic literacies.

In this chapter, we consider what the classroom of tomorrow could look like, but in doing so we draw on the teaching practices of today, using examples from teaching situations in different contexts. We return to many of the themes in previous chapters: communities of learners/communities of practice; identities/positioning; and the role of power/status in literacy teaching. We ask these questions:

- How can we use home literacy practices in the classroom?

- How can these home literacies be bridged across home and school?

- How can we change the way literacy is taught to be in tune with the identities of our students?

- How can we provide an access route to academic literacies so our students succeed in our classrooms?

WHAT IS COVERED IN THIS CHAPTER

In this chapter we look first at how to find out about the literacy practices our students engage in out of school. Then we look at new literacies, that is, digital literacies in the classroom. We then consider critical literacy as a way forward for literacy education. We consider how to combine this approach with artifactual literacies so that objects become more central to classroom literacies, as being bridging devices between home and school. Listening to students tell us about their lives is important for literacy learning and we describe some **listening methodologies** for use in classroom settings. Finally, we present new curricula for new times as well as pedagogies that speak to these new theories.

All the way through, we think about creating spaces for teachers and students to share in literacy within democratic classroom spaces. We assume that teachers and students can be in the driving seat of change, and we listen to their voices. We ensure that our examples come from all over the world, including Australia, South Africa, the USA, Canada and the UK, and we listen to the way in which these voices can shape literacy practices for the future.

RESEARCHING LITERACY PRACTICES IN THE CLASSROOM

In the vignette that begins the chapter, the teacher used dual-language books in the classroom to strong effect. She described how harnessing students' linguistic identities in the classroom had a powerful effect on reading motivation. Students also need to be *invested* in literacy practices in the classroom so they can navigate them in order to succeed in their

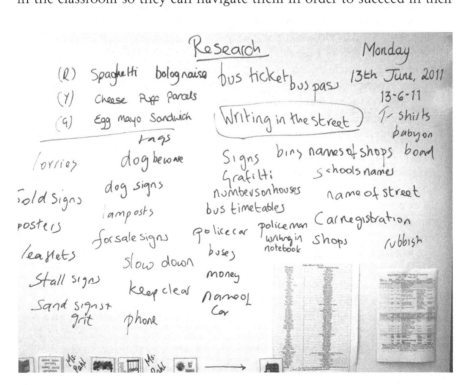

Figure 6.1 Whiteboard record of discussion

future literate identities (Norton, 2010). Many studies (e.g., Moje et al., 2004; Davies & Merchant, 2009) have begun to sketch out ways of harnessing students' home literacy practices and their digital literacies in the classroom.

- How much time do you invest in certain literacy practices over others? Where do you engage with these practices?

Below we present some examples of researching home literacy practices in classroom settings.

Vignette: Writing in the home and in the street

This project involved a group of students aged between 10 and 11 in a school in the North of England, UK. The project was concerned with the writing the children experience in the home and in the street. Kate came in, together with Steve Pool, an artist, to research the writing the children did at home and at school and in the street. The discussion that followed was lively. In Figure 6.1 on the previous page, which is a photograph of a whiteboard with a record of a discussion about writing, the students brainstormed the different kinds of writing that took place in the home, the school and in the street. Students created the categories for these domains of practice, that is, home, school and street. In school, they included in their categories of writing the teacher's 'star chart' as well as her private assessments of the children's performance at school in their literacy practices chart. The teacher was surprised to find that the children saw her writing within the same frame as their assessed writing in the classroom. The students also described writing at home, including diaries, poetry and writing to relatives who are away.

Describing and locating writing in the street precipitated a lively discussion about the graffiti that surrounded the school. The school was in an area where there was a lot of graffiti, including obscene graffiti in the children's playgrounds. Students then interviewed each other about graffiti and found that some students were concerned about the obscene graffiti surrounding their school. They were worried about their young siblings seeing the graffiti. As a result of these discussions, they decided to take a series of walks around their community to research this further. As a result of the walks, the students went to see a local police officer and asked for the graffiti to be removed. The police arranged for the graffiti to be removed, and the children felt safer in their community. They also presented a film for the local School Improvement Service about literacy in the community. They showed how difficult it was to grow up in a neighbourhood where graffiti was so obscene.

Figure 6.2 Graffiti, as recorded by children

  Points of Reflection: Understanding literacy as a
social practice in the classroom

- What literacy practices do you teach?

- Which literacy practices are valued most in the classroom?

- Why is this?

- What practices are located outside the classroom?

- What counts as literacy within the classroom?

- What other modes lie within literacy practices?

- What can you do to bridge home literacy practices with school literacy
  practices?

A good way of researching home literacies is to use disposable cameras to
create opportunities for discussion. In a small-scale research project, two
groups of primary school children were involved in investigating the use
of literacy in their lives, using disposable cameras to record literacy
events and texts. These photographs generated discussion and reflection

on what the children found. The researchers found that the children used literacy:

- as a way of maintaining and reinforcing relationships;

- as a means of organizing life;

- as a vehicle for learning;

- as reflection of identity;

- for private pleasure (Burnett & Myers, 2002: 57).

These understandings were then used to enrich teachers' understandings of the children's literacy practices, and were used in classroom activities.

 Points of Reflection: The efficacy of observation

Observation as a tool is rich in possibilities. While we cannot probe the psyche, we can use techniques such as observation and analysis of the things children make to give us insights about how thought is structured, as well as how the social organization of the world appears to the child (Pahl, 1999).

Finding out about your students' home literacy practices allows an understanding of the changing nature of literacy. If your students use text messaging, play on games consoles, engage in making *YouTube* videos, play multi-player games or browse *Facebook*, these are all new literacy practices which can be drawn upon in classroom practice.

Below we present an example by a class teacher who wanted to develop her students' writing in the classroom.

Vignette: Home school links

By Lynn Marr

My particular interest is home/school links as I am keen to engage and motivate the children in my class in order to improve their literacy skills. My belief is that if their learning becomes more personal to them, it will be relevant to them and, in effect, they will be taking more ownership of their learning and development. My ultimate aim is to inspire the children to become motivated writers. I have a Year 6 class of very mixed abilities and

I observed that they particularly love writing stories in the first person. When they wrote their own autobiographies, this really engaged them and the quality of work produced by the children was fantastic. Upon reflection, I realized that the children had a more positive attitude to their writing when they were personally involved in the content, and this then focused my attention on developing home/school links.

I discussed with the children what literacy meant to them and the many different ways in which literacy comes into our lives. Together, we then created a blank noticeboard so that the children could become actively involved in taking ownership of it. They were told that this was to be their noticeboard for 'blogging' their thoughts on notes about literacy and their interests and hobbies. The children were also allowed to bring things in from home that could be attached to the board and that they felt were linked somehow to literacy. They were all very enthusiastic about getting involved with this, and this enthusiasm continued throughout the project. I also had several discussions with children individually about the use of literacy within their lives and their home and school practices, to further my research. Conversations also took place about what was being brought in from home to pin on our noticeboard and why they thought it was important both to them and to our noticeboard. The children also talked to each other about the project and shared their thoughts and interests with the whole class. This also helped to develop good speaking and listening skills and positive relationships within the classroom.

The children became actively involved in maintaining and updating the noticeboard and the children's conversations about it enhanced their speaking and listening and social skills. While this was not obviously the main aim of my project, it was a wonderful consequence of it! The children's response to writing was noticeably more enthusiastic, particularly their ability to write descriptively (in the first person) and poetry (again, in the first person). They also completed more homework than was actually given to them, bringing in personal accounts and also pieces of writing about anything, ranging from their pets to what they did at the weekend. Above all, some children who were less motivated before this project actually started to take a pride in their writing and in their work. The children's learning began relating to them personally and collaborative learning took place within the classroom. The children's speaking and listening skills were enhanced and, ultimately, in my opinion, they became much more motivated and able writers.

In all of these examples, the children's writing was harnessed to their identities, passions and community. The classroom was opened to new ideas, and new literacies. Power relations in the classroom shifted, as the children were able to tell teachers what they saw and discovered. This way of working connects education to the outside world, and sees schools as hubs for the community. Schools can become spaces where resource networks are mapped and children can access wider research connecting them to other networks (Facer, 2011). Children live in networks, digital, human, embodied spaces, and a pedagogy that recognizes this can then support their literacy lives.

- Identify the networks in your everyday and working life. Consider, for example, spatial networks, human networks, textual networks, material networks. What do these networks enable you to do in your life?

NEW LITERACIES IN THE CLASSROOM

The shaping of the new curriculum needs to respond to the new pathways our students take through 'globalised and local, virtual and material social fields' (Luke & Carrington, 2002: 233). In the new modern world of clicking, societies connect virtually, and there is increased speed of economic movement across the globe. The way information is presented is changing and moving, as states' boundaries blur. Increased inequalities in urban spaces make it more urgent to harness the skills of young people to education and to foster their literacy development. Out-of-school literacies that researchers have documented include:

- blogs;

- wikis;

- console games playing;

- playing online games;

- communicating with others in online chat rooms;

- text messaging;

- bidding on *eBay*;

- surfing the web;

- *Facebook*;

- *Twitter*;

- *YouTube*;

- reading on Kindles.

- How can the curriculum respond to these changing times and changing textual practices?

Theory Box: Julia Davies and Guy Merchant on Web 2 for schools – learning and social participation

Julia Davies and Guy Merchant (2009) have explored ways in which children's digital literacies can be harnessed for classroom literacy. They argue that Web 2 has very different properties that, in turn, facilitates participation. Online profiles in the form of avatars can do this. Platforms such as *YouTube* encourage young people to generate their own content. Since many young people already engage in social networking practices, Web 2 is a positive platform for learning in the classroom. It is highly motivating. It also allows children to play with new identities, and also use literacy. For example, platforms such as *Second Life* facilitate sharing and communication, and a textual space. Davies and Merchant provide an example of a platform that used Web 2 for learning.

Creating virtual worlds in schools for children to use

A mini virtual world, called 'Barnsborough', specially designed for 9–11 year-old children in schools in one local authority in the UK, was set up to encourage children to use this as a platform for learning. The community that was set up was less hierarchical than in the real world and students began to explore new identities while using literacy in different ways. Davies and Merchant (2009) argue that technologies such as *Twitter*, wikis, blogs, *Facebook* and texting are all useful literacies that can be used in different ways in the classroom.

Recent innovative projects that engage with new literacies have included using *Twitter* in the classroom, as described in Chapter 3 (Bearne & Bazalgette, 2010), making films, using radio stations, making Apps and developing web platforms for *Facebook*-style interaction. These all harness young people's enthusiasm for digital literacies in reading and writing curricula.

CRITICAL LITERACY IN THE CLASSROOM

In order to make sense of new literacies, young people need to be able to recognize how different types of text work. They need both to be able to decode texts, but also to comprehend them. They also need to be able to link these texts to wider networks. These could include community networks as well as networks from the world of finance, employment and digital networks. 'Critical literacy' is a term that describes the process of making sense of texts of all kinds in relation to these wider networks. It can also include a focus on making and creating new texts that address issues that come out of this process. Faced with a plethora of advertising and commercial texts, as well as drawing on personal and community narratives, often requires students to recognize ways in which some texts discriminate against certain ideals and values. Critical literacy helps students to become alive to those processes and so create texts which celebrate their own identities and values.

In order to make sense of new texts, we would suggest using critical literacy as a framework. Muspratt et al. (1997) showed how this could be done with a focus on texts and provided a methodology for interrogating texts so that students could identify how the texts worked. They identified four approaches to texts:

- Code breaker (reading and decoding texts);

- Meaning-making (understanding meanings in texts);

- Text user (what the text does and how it does it – design and content issues);

- Text critic (critically framing text content and design) (Muspratt et al., 1997).

This helps us see what students can do with texts in the classroom. However, we have also found it useful to have a wider view of critical literacy, one that accounts for place, and for the inequalities in society that shape children's lives. It is important that literacy education is about the space for change for children's lives. In this, we are drawing on a much broader body of work that includes the work of Ernest Morrell (2008), Hilary Janks (2010), Barbara Comber (2010) and Joanne Larson and Jackie Marsh (2005). These scholars combine a focus on literacy education with an interest in how students can actively interrogate meaning-making processes so that more general inequalities can be addressed.

All these approaches are useful in educational settings. However, here we have decided to focus on one particular approach, from a participatory project called 'Designing Socially Just Learning Communities' by a teacher education group called The Literacy for Social Justice Teacher Research Group (Rogers et al., 2009). This group participated in a number of projects that worked to create real change in the communities where they worked. Here it is possible to recognize how the notion of critical literacy can become alive in community contexts. We have therefore drawn on Rogers and colleagues' (2009) critical literacy education framework, which focuses on four dimensions of critical literacy education:

- Building community;

- Developing critical stances;

- Critical inquiry and analysis;

- Action, advocacy and social change (Rogers et al., 2009: 13).

This process is circular, and can be used in literacy education. For example:

- **Building community** can involve the community walk-arounds by the children to log graffiti described earlier.

- **Developing critical stances** can include the discussions around which kind of graffiti is appropriate in which context.

- **Critical inquiry and analysis** can include the stage in which children interviewed each other about the graffiti and also reflected together on the photographs they produced.

- **Action, advocacy and social change** can include the moment when they went to the community police officer about the obscene graffiti, which resulted in its removal.

In this way, literacy education is more closely linked to neighbourhood and to social action in the community.

- How do communities organize signs? Ask students to take photographs of two signs in their community and analyze them.

In our joint work, we have also looked at the way neighbourhoods are full of objects, both material and immaterial. For example, children carry artifacts with them, such as favourite toys or books, but they also communicate online, and sometimes this communication vanishes on screen. In this way, however, literacy can become more situated. We suggest that focusing on objects in homes and communities is a useful way of understanding neighbourhoods. For example, treasured objects in homes call up stories that tell of experiences that often are different from the stories we hear on the news. They are often intergenerational. They often relate to objects that have little value but are imbued with personal meanings. Children have favourite objects that travel with them. These objects can be written about in school. We have called this approach 'Artifactual Literacies' (Pahl & Rowsell, 2010).

Theory Box: Kate Pahl and Jennifer Rowsell on artifactual literacies

In our joint work (Pahl & Rowsell, 2010), we have argued for the use of objects or artifacts as a way of changing the power relations between students and teachers in the classroom. Artifacts position learners differently. When you bring an object into the classroom, the object can be talked about in relation to identity and to its material qualities. Moving from private, lived spaces to the public domains of schooling, artifacts can give participants a place in schooling and move them into content area literacy. This process can be extended to include ways of using objects or artifacts with students in the classroom. If a focus on artifacts, and the relationship between objects and stories, is developed, together with a focus on critical literacy, it is possible to reshape how power relations work in the classroom. Artifacts can be focused on in the classroom to create a discussion of these themes. Teachers can then discuss an object's:

- value;

- timescale;

- space and place;

- production;

- mode.

Certain stories become more important, such as stories of handed-down objects, and things that matter to people. This positions people differently.

We have used this framework to suggest a pedagogy of **artifactual critical literacy**. In the following section, we unpack how this pedagogy can work in the classroom.

ARTIFACTUAL CRITICAL LITERACIES

Building community

The concept of 'building community' could include a focus on everyday routines and practices. Teachers could ask children to take pictures of everyday objects to bring into the classroom. Students and teachers could create small exhibitions of these objects, and develop writing and oral storytelling around these objects.

Theory Box: Mary Scanlan on My Story in a Box

In a research study in Bristol, students (aged 5–6) were asked to fill a shoe-box with objects that related to themselves and their lives. A letter went home with the shoebox asking for objects as varied as Christmas decorations or soft toys. They were then asked to bring these objects into the classroom and describe these to their classmates and then write about them. The other students were also more inspired by listening to their classmates. Children expressed a wider range of feelings and emotions. The teacher found that students' writing was more expressive, and included much more powerful accounts of experience. Shy students were also more expressive, both orally and in their writing, when describing their special objects. Object boxes are important bridges between home and school (Scanlan, 2010).

This approach can also be used to foster listening between students and teachers so that students whose voices are less heard in the classroom can claim space. In some ways, an artifactual approach to literacy created new, more equal roles between student and teacher.

- Bring in your own artifacts and have students sort them into genres and stories (see Chapter 2).

Objects can also be used to develop critical stances in classroom settings:

Building critical stances

Building critical stances using an artifactual literacies approach can begin by students bringing in artifacts to interrogate using a critical literacies framework. As an exercise, objects can be interrogated for their meanings in relation to what kinds of values are attached to particular objects and why. Different objects can be considered in relation to their value, the timescale attached to them, their production, mode, and relation to institutions of power. Objects then become visible in different ways. Language is important to create criticality. By presenting different objects in different languages, it is possible to consider ways in which certain languages privilege certain meanings over others.

Critical inquiry and analysis

Critical inquiry and analysis can stem from analyzing artifacts in such an interrogating way. Artifacts have their own pedagogic potential in offering ways of telling stories, but they can also be placed within different settings to create juxtapositions that then inform learning in new ways. The movement from critical stance to critical inquiry can be afforded through a programme that develops a more sustained approach to artifactual critical literacy.

 Activity

For example, teachers and students can create *Facebook* profiles of characters in literary works, which can compel students to think in character.

- Who would engage in conversations in a wall space?
- What is a character's favourite novel?
- What is his or her favourite saying?

Thinking in character through contemporary social networking or digital communities of practice (Lave & Wenger, 1991) builds on skills students carry with them from hours spent online using *Twitter*, *MySpace* or *Facebook*. In terms of thinking artifactually, creating *Facebook* pages for characters not only forces students to think in terms of literary characters, but also to think about stuff, objects, artifacts that they value. How would they visually mediate themselves? What kinds of multimodal rhetorical devices might they invoke to mediate their identities? Literary worlds can be lifted out by combining the digital and the artifactual.

Action, advocacy and social change

Artifactual critical literacy can include a focus on social change through artifacts. For example, a group of families created a museum exhibition, with a curator, about their favourite objects. This exhibition was also turned into a website by the artist, Zahir Rafiq, called 'Every Object Tells A Story' (see www.everyobjecttellsastory.org.uk). This included a teaching resource pack that used this methodology in family learning settings. These innovative practices opened up the families' home spaces and linked them to wider spaces of objects, stories and a recognition of the similarities across cultural spaces – as all of us have valued objects and stories.

Points of Reflection

If we conceptualize critical artifactual literacy as being about creating new spaces but drawing on the old to make the new, the following ideas could be developed:

• Bringing artifactual literacy into the classroom – redesigning the classroom to reflect the reality of the outside world;

• Using artifacts to create social change (e.g., developing a campaign on school closure through creating digital artifacts that tell the story of the school);

• Moving the school into the community by creating an exhibition of artifacts and stories;

• Using local spaces as resources for learning and developing resources that occupy a 'third space', jointly owned by parents, students, community members and teachers.

Ultimately, this involves recognizing the power of narrative when thinking about artifactual critical literacy. The power of artifacts to create a space for listening has immense resonance in this field. Teaching artifactual literacy is about finding a place in the classroom for these stories. It also involves adopting a listening methodology to enable students' voices to be heard in new ways.

Theory Box: Alison Clark and Peter Moss on the Mosaic Approach

Alison Clark, with her colleague Peter Moss, developed the Mosaic Approach to develop a methodology that listened to young children (Clark et al. 2005). This methodology involved using a mosaic of methods to gain

(Cont'd)

children's perspectives using their own modal choices. These methods are:

- multi-method, that is, recognizes the different voices of children;

- participatory: treating children as experts in their own right;

- reflexive: including children and parents in reflecting on meanings;

- adaptable, that is, can be applied in a number of contexts and institutions;

- focused on children's lived experiences;

- embedded into practice, that is, it can be used to evaluate but also to inform early years practice (Clark et al., 2005: 31).

For example, child-led tours around schools, drawing, map-making and using digital cameras elicited a much more complex account of lived experience in school than just oral talk. In her work on listening, Alison Clark also found that a further stage, which involves a process of reflecting on what children have produced with children, enabled a deeper understanding of children's meanings as they were produced, and enabled them to be recognized in the context in which they were produced. She divided the process of doing this into three stages:

- Stage One: Gathering children and adults' perspectives;

- Stage Two: Discussing (reviewing) the material;

- Stage Three: Deciding on areas of continuity and change (Clark, 2010: 42).

Architects and planners could then access these meanings when making decisions about children's spaces. More importantly, children could have a say in these decisions, and in a shared research space, and could become actors in a process of creating shared meanings.

- What might a mosaic approach for literacy education look like?

It might include children doing the following:

- Using cameras to take photographs of literacy practices;

- Making maps of their local area;

- Brainstorming literacy practices in groups;

- Walking through the neighbourhood with digital recording equipment;

- Writing about literacy practices;

- Reflecting on these different sources of data;

- Making a film about this experience;

- Presenting the film to key people (e.g., school inspectors);

- Developing a new research proposal together.

The idea of children as researchers is not new. However, we would suggest that children can become involved in all stages of research. These would include:

- drafting and finalizing a research proposal;

- deciding on the research questions;

- collecting the data;

- analyzing the data;

- writing up the project;

- presenting the project.

In the following example, students were able to co-write a book about the effects of gentrification on a particular neighbourhood – in this case, Harlem.

Theory Box: Valerie Kinloch – 'Harlem on our Minds'

Valerie Kinloch (2010) worked with a group of students from Harlem High School to explore the literacies of the young students who lived in Harlem and attended the school. Through this process, the students and Valerie charted the gentrification of Harlem. The students began to write about this process and these were included in the book.

(Cont'd)

Kinloch and the co-writers, Phillip and Khaleeq, described the literacies of Harlem, historically, geographically and in terms of the identities of the young people growing up in Harlem. Kinloch walked with young people through the neighbourhood, and as she walked, she heard their stories. Phillip and Khaleeq articulated how they felt about the experience of watching their neighbourhood change.

In Valerie's work, literacy is linked to the experience of place and space and is critically important as a weapon used to fight ways in which Harlem's heritage as a site for Black culture was being undermined by gentrification.

We therefore think of literacy as being historically, geographically and spatially located.

- Think of a key historical event in your community. Can you locate your students' literacies in relation to these events? Can you link their everyday spaces and literacy practices to these wider historical events?

We turn to examples that involve 'place-making' as a source of strength. New spatial literacies approaches understand the need to include space as a resource for meaning-making. For example, Barbara Comber describes how a class worked to resist climate change by creating an environmental project (Comber, 2010).

Theory Box: Barbara Comber on critical multiliteracies in place

Barbara Comber (2010) presented a project called 'Learnscapes' based in a school, where students are looking at environmental impact. To explore this theme, the students animated and designed multimodal texts as well as engaged with real-life artefacts, such as a bird hide.

These projects were profoundly rooted in the place and space in which the school was situated as well as the new challenges of climate change and the need for sustainable literacies. In one of the examples, a school where a number of sustainable literacy projects were taking place, Comber emphasized the artifactual nature of the project, as evidenced in the 'non-school like features' which were manifested in the material:

Interestingly this school has many non-school-like features, the chook shed, the trading table, the outside classroom, the half-made bird hide, the wood-pile, the gallery of student work on outdoor surfaces and fences, ribbons keeping people out of a natural scrub area under regeneration. (Comber, 2010: 54)

In this project there is a combining of a focus on environmental communicative practices together with a multiliteracies perspective, which takes in the idea of students as active designers of meaning and environmental campaigners in a situated, place-infused context. Comber (2010) describes this approach within her projects as one of 'critical multiliteracies'.

We have used Comber's work, together with our artifactual literacies approach, to develop a lens to look at literacy in communities. By bringing artifactual literacies together with place-based pedagogy, as well as an understanding of the realities of inequality within communities, a more *situated* model of critical literacies is born, one that is both artifactual *and* place-based. This form of critical literacy is active, questioning, and directly concerned with social change.

We have considered ways of researching literacy and drawing research into pedagogy. We have also discussed ways of providing ownership of the classroom space by bringing new thoughts and ideas into the space through the use of objects. We have then considered listening methodologies and finding new ways to share ideas and create critical spaces for thinking about possible worlds.

Shaping new ideas using a critical literacy framework also leads us to consider the ways in which change can happen. In the final section, we turn to the framework that is 'curricula'.

CHANGING CURRICULA FOR CHANGING TIMES

We think of curriculum as something that comes from society, that is, constructed socially, and is derived through social events and social meanings. Curricula are shaped by theories of how literacy is taught. Often, they are shaped by what kind of literacy is thought to be important. In many countries, literacy is seen as a set of transferable skills, to be transferred and disseminated.

- Do curricula objectives match or mirror what we actually do? Are they linked or are they not linked to the real world of texts?

Curricula are shaped by power. What is taught and how literacy is taught are often determined by people in government who would like to see students learn a particular form of literacy. These forms of literacy tend to be academic literacies, characterized by specific ways of speaking and writing. They are very often positioned differently from other forms of literacy. *Facebook*, for example, is rarely seen as an academic literacy in the classroom, even though it is a literacy practice. The academic essay is seen as an academic literacy, even though it is rarely used in everyday life.

Theory Box: Allan Luke and Vic Carrington on understanding the curriculum in the context of twenty-first-century communicational practices

Luke and Carrington (2002) argue that there needs to be a critical understanding of the shape of literacy that is emerging in everyday contexts within schooling. The current curriculum is, in many countries, adapted to fit an earlier model of print-literacy, and does not fit with the changing contemporary communicational landscape. Rather than curriculum practice being about 'fetishing the teaching of basic print skills' (2002: 248), it could be about an understanding of broader contexts that engage with the new communicational realities. Their argument is that a critical literacy standpoint can deliver the beginnings of this understanding. This standpoint also requires a recognition of the shifts in communication that have taken place.

Part of the difficulty of curricula is that they are founded upon policy-makers' concepts of literacy and what literacy practices should be salient in the spaces of school. These concepts are based upon schema gathered from childhood about which kinds of literacy practices count.

 Activity

Sedimenting Subjectivities in Teaching

Think about how your own subjectivity impacts on your teaching practice and your teaching philosophy. Find five pedagogic texts that you use in your teaching, for example:

- a sample lesson;
- a textbook;

- a page from your agenda or diary;

- a professional reading;

- a rubric that you use or made.

Now, lift out parts of the pedagogic texts that signify you and your subjectivities – your beliefs, your values, your interests, your culture, your race, your religion, etc. Now put post-it notes or use a marker to highlight these aspects of your subjectivities (hint, perhaps use different coloured markers to signal different big 'D' discourses or subjectivities). Now think about ways of using this same lens on student work. What aspects are different and what are the same?

However, literacy practices are changing. In the theory box below, we explore how teachers' acquired ways of being, their attitudes in relation to popular culture, structure their curricula choices. These choices then restrict what they can teach children, as the teachers censor out their own experience of popular culture and make school a place that does not relate to young children's out-of-school interests and passions.

Theory Box: Jackie Marsh on pre-service teachers and popular cultural literacies

Jackie Marsh analyzed pre-service teachers' attitudes to popular culture. She used the concept of 'habitus' from Bourdieu (1990), meaning an acquired set of dispositions that are carried from childhood. She asked the question:

- How do pre-service teachers construct the curriculum using their habitus?

Marsh (2006) analyzed how a Bourdieusian framework of field, together with habitus, and with the concept of doxa, which is the dynamic between the two, is key in helping us to understand how the curriculum is shaped by these relations of power. 'Doxa describes the practice that results when habitus and field are attuned' (2006: 164).

Marsh then used these concepts to analyze the relationship between primary teachers' beliefs in relation to popular culture and the literacy curriculum. She argued that pre-service teachers tended to try to match what they thought would be the expectations of the school, and often buried their own knowledge of popular culture in relation to their practice in school. Curriculum, then, should be shaped by the societal demands of a changing communicational context.

Part of the task for literacy educators is to unpack the 'schema' of literacy that you hold. Thinking about the uses of literacy in everyday life can call up the 'schema' that we use, the 'ways with words' (Heath, 1983) that are everyday. This thinking is important in recognizing how the students we teach may experience literacy in profoundly different, but as important, ways.

 Points of Reflection

Think back to your early experience of literacy.

- Did it involve books or oral stories?
- What were your favourite texts?
- Were they oral or written?
- Did you have a computer in your home?
- How early did you access Web 2 and develop the skills to create blogs and wikis?
- What artifacts were associated with literacy when you were a child?
- Did you include moving-image media in your thinking about literacy?
- How much did you enjoy television or *YouTube*?
- How savvy were you as a child with new technologies?

Our discussion of literacy now has to incorporate the new 'mindsets' (Lankshear & Knobel, 2006) that accompany new literacies. Now you can do an audit of out-of-school literacies in your classroom.

Students can help unpack the schemas they have of literacy and the ways they think about their out-of-school literacy practices. Sometimes these literacies seem invisible and are not 'counted' as literacy, for example, the literacy associated with virtual worlds such as Club Penguin. Students might use texts, and read and write without badging this activity as 'literacy'. A theory of curriculum in new times needs to unite a critical literacy perspective together with an understanding of these new literacies. Below, we consider new curricula and pedagogies in literacy education and think about how these can work for classroom teachers. In all of this, we put the theory into this book into practice, and help make the theory and thinking come alive.

NEW CURRICULA AND PEDAGOGIES IN LITERACY EDUCATION

In this section we offer practical examples of curriculum and pedagogy in these new times. We consider critical literacy as well as how to make this work in the classroom. We include ideas on assessment and on portfolios for students. We also consider pedagogical concepts such as third space theory to bring students' home literacies into the classroom. We also look at how a multimodal approach to literacy can aid this process. Finally, we put forward a Curriculum Framework, which we have taken from New Brunswick, in Canada, that enacts some of these ideas.

We have seen how, in order to look at texts, a critical literacy lens is useful. This lens might think about ways in which texts create assumptions and develop ideologies. Pedagogies that draw on critical literacy are effective in harnessing students to academic literacies while drawing on their own research and funds of knowledge.

Theory Box: Ernest Morrell on critical literacies in place

Ernest Morrell (2008) and his colleagues created opportunities for urban high school students to engage in writing through a series of seminars in which the students used notebooks to record their experiences, note down their journeys as critical researchers, and write a personal letter to someone who inspired them. They also crafted an issue piece to a policy-maker. The students engaged in real-life research projects, spending time 'in the field' in streets, neighbourhoods and schools. They used Geographic Information Systems to map the distribution of liquor stores (off-licences) to libraries in one area, finding out that in one area there were 58 liquor stores and one library in a high-density area. Students also made films and presented PowerPoint presentations at the end of the seminar process. The students then presented their work at major conferences, including the American Educational Research Association conference.

The use of the composition notebooks was critical in encouraging the production of research methodologies and to record fieldnotes and researcher journeys as well as interviews, and then do data analysis. These books could be drawn upon in presentations. The students learned to 'do' academic literacy while at the same time researching in new ways their neighbourhoods and their local communities. Rather than 'other' the world, these students were both part of the world, yet aimed to change it. Morrell's work sees critical literacy as integral to the process of social transformation and civic participation (Morrell, 2008).

As readers and writers, we engage with texts in a fashion which is personal and ideological. We are not value-free. By looking at what lies beneath texts, we acknowledge the way in which they are traces of social practice. They are constructed by agencies and people, and developed over a timeframe. Sometimes texts can be identified with particular, more settled forms, which we recognize in everyday life, for example, formal letters or newspaper articles. At other times, texts are unstable and can move rapidly in and out of speech-like forms of text and more written forms of text. **Weblogs**, for example, move between informal discourse and more formal written forms.

One way of thinking about critical literacy is as a way into pedagogy. That is, as a space where teachers and students can 'crack the codes' together. For example, Hilary Janks (2010) gives a practical account of how this can be done in her book *Literacy and Power*. She argues for a synthesis of critical literacy education that brings together both 'school' literacy and the diverse literacies around us.

Theory Box: Hilary Janks on a critical literacy synthesis

Hilary Janks (2010), in her synthesis of critical literacy education, talks about:

- Domination – that is, the concept of language as a way of maintaining dominant modes of reproduction;

- Access – that is, the question of providing access to dominant modes of language, i.e., academic literacies;

- Diversity – that is, the different literacy practices that there are in the world;

- Design – that is, the process of production and the assembling of semiotic resources to make meaning (Janks, 2010).

Janks argues that 'we need to find ways of holding all of these elements in productive tension to achieve what is a shared goal of all critical literacy work: equity and social justice' (Janks, 2010: 27). Janks argues that critical literacy needs to be part of a much broader framework that is flexible and attuned to both the playfulness and seriousness of literacy education.

However, the reality is that students need to be credited for the work they do in school. What does getting better at critical literacy look like? How can they achieve more by using this way of learning? We will now move to the question of assessment and considerations of what getting better at critical literacy looks like.

Points of Reflection: Assessing critical literacy development

How do teachers assess critical literacy in the classroom? To assess students' critical literacy development, you can apply the following criteria:

- **Meaning-making**: the use of all resources possible in their production of texts (i.e., enabling/affording versus constraining meaning based on the genre). Do they know the practices required to build and construct cultural meanings in texts?

- **Text participant**: this is making meaning from texts. Students then ask 'What does this mean?'

- **Text user**: this is 'cracking the code' of the text, and accessing the embodied meanings in a text. How can we look at what lies beneath the text?

- **Text analyst**: this tests proficiency in the practices required to analyze, critique and second-guess texts. How can we empower students to apply critical literacies skills to texts?

Recent work (for example, Morrell, 2008) has argued for the use of notebooks or scrapbooks, in which students record their own field-notes, document in visual forms their learning journeys and develop models of writing that go beyond formal, assessed forms. These journals need not even be read by teachers. Writing journals can be used by students as private records of personal thoughts, including poetry, letters and diaries. One way to develop these forms of writing for assessment is the use of portfolios. With Virtual Learning Environments (VLEs) these can also be developed online and become **e-portfolios**.

ASSESSING NEW LITERACY STUDIES THROUGH PORTFOLIOS AND E-PORTFOLIOS

To assess your students' literacy development when working within a New Literacy Studies/critical literacies framework, students can be encouraged to create a portfolio as an effective way of helping them to invest in the literacy process. This can also be created online in a Virtual Learning Environment, and can be called an e-portfolio. At the beginning of the year, each student receives a portfolio/web page that they can decorate however they like. As a culminating assessment task, ask students to divide their portfolio into sections or folders online as a collection of assignments. For example, students can provide an assignment or artifact that exhibits proficiency in speaking, listening, writing, reading, and visual communication. Students can include *YouTube* videos and PowerPoint presentations in their e-portfolio, plus use software such as Prezi to present new ideas. Structuring portfolios in relation to themes such as 'best design' or 'best piece of writing within a genre' helps students develop a greater understanding of the possibilities and constraints of contemporary curricula and activities that can grow out of the New Literacy Studies. For example, students can present artifacts in digital images that illustrate home–school literacy practices, multimodal literacies, or artifacts of their identity.

Another way of structuring the portfolio process might be based on text genres: fiction, poetry, websites, non-fiction, videogames, game cards, and so on. Portfolio note headings can reflect the learning process by looking at:

- What I knew;

- What I wanted to find out;

- What I found out;

- Reflection and analysis;

- New directions for research.

Students reflect on the process of creating artifacts to consolidate their learning. These reflections appear in each portfolio section. Portfolios represent informal forms of assessment that allow students to take ownership of their literacy development while at the same time drawing on ideas from the New Literacy Studies, such as the idea of literacy as a social practice.

> Within portfolios students can include CDs, embed links to Urls or *YouTube* videos, visual portfolios such as scrapbooks and written portfolios such as composition notebooks. Ownership of these artifacts is crucial. The portfolios can then be used to prepare presentations, and make change happen at local and national level. The portfolios are ways of organising sites of knowledge and creating a network of knowledge exchange and participation. They can also be used to create *wikis*, Blogs and *Facebook* pages. If they are presented online, they can be shared online and students can comment on each other's work in a safe virtual learning environment. Students can consider the different affordances of

different modal choices and work out the 'best fit' for their particular message. In this way, they can incorporate design choices into their work. (Sheridan & Rowsell, 2010)

- How can you draw on everyday texts for literacy in your e-portfolio, for example for screen savers and favourite websites? Think about why you like a particular image and what it does for you.

PEDAGOGIES THAT SUPPORT STUDENTS: FUNDS OF KNOWLEDGE AND THIRD SPACE

Part of the challenge for teachers is to find pedagogies that support these ways of working. Here we return to Moll's concept of **funds of knowledge**. This research emphasizes the importance of what students and communities bring to schools in terms of literacy practices (Moll et al., 1992; Gonzalez et al., 2005). These models see out-of-school literacy practices as flowing into school and developing within classrooms.

In this discussion, the focus on curricula change is to weight the knowledge in favour of the discourses and practices of students from different cultural contexts and spaces. These everyday understandings can be channelled into different forms of knowledge and can be used for academic literacies. Moll et al. (1992) and then Gutiérrez et al. (1999) and Moje et al. (2004) have suggested that these cultural resources can be used to support students to develop stronger understandings of the world, both in classrooms and everyday lives (Gutiérrez et al., 1999). As seen in Chapter 3, the term third space can be used to describe a bridge between community/home ways of speaking, reading and writing and school-based literacy practices. This third space is a space where students can be supported to move their literacy practices into a schooled, 'academic' domain of knowledge (Street, 2005). From this theory, many researchers have thought about what could be used from everyday literacy practices to support school knowledge.

How do we transform our students' funds of knowledge in classroom settings? Teachers can mediate classroom experiences for their students, bringing in a host of cultural experience from their students' funds of knowledge, and they can meet their students half-way, with a shared space in which both can participate.

Theory Box: Rachael Levy on reading in the third space

Levy (2011) used the conception of third space theory to describe how nursery-aged children in her study created a third space between home and school for the purposes of continuity in their constructions of reading. In Levy's study, the children used various elements of their home life, specifically television texts, popular culture, computer technology and play, to integrate their reading experiences at home with the primary school curriculum. Levy shows quite clearly that children draw upon the discourses of school and home in forming constructions of reading. Findings reveal that many of the children were identified as constructing a third space in their emergent literacy between home and school. For example, one of the children, Shaun, was able to use phonics at home and, at school, enjoyed his reading scheme books in both domains. At home, he was also a fluent user of digital technology. Shaun transferred his digital skills from one medium or setting to another, thus showing how he could comfortably merge 'first space' discourses (home) with 'second space' discourses (school) to create a 'third space' which was both home and school.

CURRICULUM, MULTIMODAL TEXTS AND LITERACY PRACTICES

Finally, we consider how different curricula can support children's multimodal literacies and develop their literacy skills in relation to a wider definition of literacy, one that is connected to a number of different modal choices. Drawing on our thinking in Chapter 2, when we saw how literacy could be seen to be meshed within a wide range of modalities, now we consider how curricula can support those modal choices and develop a space for children to improve their meaning-making.

Eve Bearne (2003) argued that it is possible to recognize how children draw on different *affordances* in relation to their texts. Affordances are the possibilities within texts to create meaning. Some affordances may be located in language and literacy, that is, they may be found in written texts. However, some may be drawn, but spatially organized to add to the writing. Bearne argued that we need to credit these spatial assemblages of thought, to create, in Elaine Millard's words, 'a **literacy of fusion**' – one that combines an understanding of literacy in relation to reading and writing with an understanding of literacy in relation to images (Millard, 2003). Multimodality can be used within the classroom in a variety of ways to support students' learning.

One model for thinking about meaning-making is the multiliteracies framework (Cope & Kalantzis, 2000). This involves teaching literacy by looking at the ways in which students move through these stages:

- Situated practice;

- Overt instruction;

- Critical framing;

- Transformed practice.

It is possible to see how the students can take a rap song and make sense of it in new ways. A knowledge of students' new literacies makes that possible.

Cope and Kalantzis offer the following classroom vignette:

Vignette: Putting multiliteracies to the test

Back to Australia again, and this time to William Ross High School in Townsville, North Queensland. This is another of the schools with which we were working in our Language Australia/ARC project. Here Fran Hodges is working with her Year 9 English class on video clips. She starts by presenting the students with the lyrics of a Toni Childs' song. All the devices and conventions of poetry are to be found as well as the specific conventions of song lyrics, such as a repeated chorus. Then she plays the CD. She asks what the music adds to the lyrics and how it does it. Then she plays the video clip. She asks how the imagery of the clip and gestures of the singer add to the meaning of the song. The students have now completed an analysis of the multimodal grammar of the song. Next, the students bring in their favourite songs.

Situated practice: Students bring music they relate to in their own life experience and immerse themselves in the music of their friends.

Overt instruction: Fran works with the students as they develop a grammar which analyzes the linguistic, audio and visual design of the songs and their video clips.

Critical framing: Students compare the meanings and the cultures they represent – the song of the white woman (Toni Childs) rap, techno, house, reggae, heavy metal or whatever.

Transformed practice: The students write, perform and make a video clip for a song they have written themselves. (Cope & Kalatantzis, 2004)

DRAWING ON STUDENTS' NEW LITERACIES

In the previous examples, the curriculum has been reshaped to support students' new literacies. For example, a group of researchers worked with a school in Australia to assist with the under-achievement of certain groups in the school. A core of 25 per cent of the children in the school struggled with literacy. The researchers did an audit of the skills these students already had, and discovered they had strong social networks within the community, in-depth local knowledge about the demography and culture of their own community, interest in money and sports, and how to deal with difficult economic circumstances (Luke & Carrington, 2002). They also had extensive knowledge of popular culture, music, fashion and youth culture, computer and videogames, Internet surfing and the new technologies. The researchers worked with the teachers to audit and develop classroom strategies which built on these strengths. The researchers worked to bring together:

> ... a richer, more intellectually demanding and 'contemporary' analysis of these kids' identities and competencies, a more cogent understanding of the overlapping and multiple communities that these children inhabit with a balanced focus on code breaking, meaning making, using texts in everyday life and critical literacy. (Luke & Carrington, 2002: 243)

The new curriculum could take a number of shapes, including:

- Using the Internet to audit and to analyze global flows of work;

- Using writing and online communication to participate with virtual communities linked to current interests;

- Reading multiple literary texts that generate or engage intercultural and contrastive historical perspectives (Luke & Carrington, 2002: 247).

Curricula change can focus on both the local and the global, drawing on children's identities and interests, and allowing a space for them to grow and develop that is at once embedded and inclusive.

CURRICULUM, PEDAGOGY AND NEW LITERACY STUDIES

One model of curriculum that takes in New Literacy Studies, critical literacies, multimodality and local and global literacies is the New Brunswick

Curriculum Framework, which was produced by researchers and educators in Canada. Below, we present the key elements of this framework, as it relates to literacy:

Theory Box: The Early Years Curriculum Framework for New Brunswick

The Curriculum Framework has a section on communication and literacies in which it states that:

> Children communicate right from birth. Sounds, silences, pauses, gestures, movement, eye contact, and body language, our first modes of communication, stay with us throughout our lifetimes. Children interpret and re-invent their worlds using multiple forms of communication and representation.

This Curriculum acknowledges diversity and difference across a range of communicative practices:

> Children learn to express, represent and interpret their feelings, ideas and questions through speaking, listening, reading, writing, dancing, singing, drawing, moving, and constructing. They learn a wide range of literate practices through their interactions with others and within particular social and cultural contexts. Being literate no longer simply means the ability to read and write. Being literate means negotiating a wide range of literate practices across various communities.

The Framework acknowledges that literacy itself has changed:

> What it means to be literate changes over time, place, and within and across cultures. In the twenty-first-century technological innovations are shifting the meaning of being literate from a dominant focus on language and print to a more multimodal focus. Multimodal literacies involve the simultaneous use of the modes of image, print, gaze, gesture, movement, speech and/or sound effects. Reading picture books, fiction and non-fiction, is one of the most accessible and popular multimodal forms of literacy engagement. Singing, painting, dramatic play, television and computers represent others.

Above all, the Framework describes the way in which literacy is part of community and social identities:

> Through their participation in various contexts, children contribute to changes in what it means to be literate. This is because they are active rather than passive learners in the process of making sense of

(Cont'd)

their worlds. They both influence and are influenced by language and literacy practices in their homes, neighbourhoods and wider communities. Children's personal, social and literate identities are co-constructed in their interactions with others, and by the expectations – for example, gendered expectations – held by others. Children's creations and productions tell us who they think they are and who they might like to be.

The Framework is therefore divided into three facets:

- Communicative practices;

- Multimodal meaning-making;

- Literate identities with/in communities.

Within these facets children are encouraged to create texts reflective of family, local, and global literacies, learn various local literacy practices within a range of communities together with an understanding of the uniqueness and similarities of their family literacies and those of others. Children are encouraged to transport the literacies of popular culture from home into the centre, as well as explore identities from characters embedded in popular culture as well as grow in their knowledge of the multifaceted practices of their local communities. From this, a critical understanding can be developed of new digital literate practices, and the ability to make sense of these texts can emerge (Early Education and Care: English Curriculum Framework for New Brunswick, 2007: 30–31).

This curriculum framework brings in multimodal and digital texts and focuses on family literacies as a grounding for schooled literacies. New curricula and pedagogies have to account for diversity both in the way the frameworks are set up and in relation to thinking about theory and practice.

 Activity

Think about diversity in your practice. Ask students to deconstruct a policy document. Ask them to think about these questions:

- Whose voices are presented in the document?

- Is the document accessible?

- Are the visuals sympathetic to a diverse community?

- Whose language is privileged?

- Whose voices are not present within the document?

Here we return to Joanne Larson and Jackie Marsh's (2005) work to think about diversity in thinking through pedagogy and curriculum.

Theory Box: Joanne Larson and Jackie Marsh on critical literacy across frameworks

In their book *Making Literacy Real* (2005), Larson and Marsh present a model that includes four different frameworks:

- New Literacy Studies (Literacy as situated, learners focus on literacy events and practices);

- Techno-literacy (Learners draw on existing competencies, but in new settings);

- Critical Literacy (Learners are positioned as active agents and critique existing textual practices, producing new texts in the process);

- Socio-cultural historical theory (Learners are active in constructing goals with a participatory framework).

Larson and Marsh argue that it is important to create a space where there is a constant interplay between these theoretical positions and practice so that students and teachers and researchers can exchange knowledge in an equitable and transformative space (Larson & Marsh, 2005).

Re-visioning literacy education is hard; however, all these examples show that if we place children and young people at the heart of the process of creating change, and given them agency, they also do 'schooled literacy' better, as the vignette below shows us.

Vignette: Reading Agents, a project in Rotherham

Inspire Rotherham is a project that aimed to improve literacy and involve the whole community in reading, in Rotherham, UK. 'Reading Agents' is a project that is led by children in schools. In each class, six children were chosen to be Reading Agents. They received a special badge and a

(Cont'd)

notebook. Their task was to improve the school library but also to research reading within the school. Children worked in groups to select books for their school library. They looked at catalogues to decide what kind of books to get. They worked with other children to select and review a wide range of books. Once they had a plan and had decided on which books to buy, they went to the bookstore to buy the books for the school. They were also given the responsibility to choose furnishings for the library, including comfortable seating and spaces to read.

As part of the project children became researchers into reading. Children constructed research questions and asked their peers about what kinds of spaces they would like for reading. They also investigated digital reading, and in some schools, children preferred to read on Kindles rather than use books.

The children decided on a methodology. They constructed questionnaires and conducted interviews with other children to find out what books they enjoyed reading. In order to find out what reading meant to the children, they asked these questions:

- How does reading make you feel?

- Does it develop your reading skills, reading more everyday?

- How does all this reading add to your own learning?

- Does it build up your confidence?

- How will all this help us in the future?

- Would you rather read your own book or a Kindle?

- Do you read more at home now?

- Did you feel you were learning when you were reading to younger children?

- Has reading influenced your life?

- What is your favourite book you've read and why?

As a result of this research, the school took action. New library scanning systems were ordered which used fingerprints to scan a book in or out. Children could then become school librarians. The schools became hubs for reading. Children read to animals in the school (especially goldfish), to younger students in the schools and were more enthusiastic about visiting a school library with bean bags, comfy seats and colour coding of books into different genres, for example, scary books, books about animals, etc. The project was targeted especially at reluctant readers. As a result of this project, boys, pupils who have English as a second language and reluctant readers improved in reading, particularly in areas of socio-economic deprivation in Rotherham.

- Can you think about a topic you could research with your students? What would happen if they decided on the topic and constructed the research themselves? How would this be a different kind of activity?

CONCLUSION

In this chapter, we have introduced exciting work going on all over the world. From South Africa we have learned about Hilary Janks' model of critical literacy, which synthesizes different conceptual frameworks to give students a handle on texts. In the context of South Africa, this is vital to give a voice to students traditionally not visible within power structures.

From the United States we have had a window into Ernest Morrell's work with high school students to create notebooks as they carry out research into out-of-school and community contexts. We have also drawn on Rebecca Rogers, Melissa Moseley, Mary Ann Kramer and the Literacy for Social Justice Teacher Research Group for an action research approach to critical literacy education.

From Australia we have heard about the work of the multiliteracies team, particularly that of Bill Cope and Mary Kalantzis, and also about Barbara Comber's work on critical literacies and place. We also refer back to the pioneering work of Peter Freebody and Allan Luke in creating a framework for critical literacy education. We presented the New Brunswick Curriculum Framework in Canada as an example of a curriculum framework that is alive to students' literate identities, their out-of-school diverse literacy practices and the forms of literacy as literacy is embedded in wider multimodal semiotic representations. Scholars such as Jackie Marsh and Joanne Larson, as well as Anne Haas Dyson, Rachel Levy, Julia Davies and Guy Merchant have showed us how teachers have worked with and mediated these new literacy practices in ways that honour children's meaning-making processes in and out of school.

At the heart of this chapter is hope. Hope that the children of tomorrow will be given space to learn in a pedagogical setting which respects their literacy practices, and affords them instruction which draws on those practices. This requires the development of an equitable classroom. Hope also that teachers are given the support to give their students this space, and are themselves given space as the mediators of the curriculum of tomorrow. This requires a flexible and adaptable curriculum. This chapter also hopes that the diverse, complex, multimodal, critical and situated literacy practices we have observed in classrooms may be enshrined in the curricula documents of the twenty-first-century.

Conclusion to the second edition of *Literacy And Education*

In this conclusion we reflect on what the field of literacy has brought and what we have learned from current research that advances the field further. We think about what literacy looks like now and what literacy will look like in the future. When we consider research on literacy we realize that much of literacy is distributed in space and time. We also realize that literacy is situated, and can disempower as well as empower communities. It is material and it can be expressed in different forms. Understanding literacy involves a sensuous engagement with the world, and a sense of literacy that is 'in place' (Pink, 2009).

- What are our visions for literacy in the future?

First, we think that literacy will be about ecologies and networks. Rather than think of individualized 'homes' which are separately resourced, resources will be developed that can be used by communities in hubs. Local libraries will become literacy networks, and ways of using libraries in different ways, as in community gardens, resource centres for food, cooking and trips, as well as spaces for literacy and art activities, will be ways forward. Schools likewise will become networked into communities in new ways, drawing on the expertise of all adults in the community, as Keri Facer (2011) has outlined.

Second, we think literacy will be seen as more embodied and sensuous. The impact on emotions of seeing negative print, either in the form of obscene graffiti or in relation to a newspaper that denigrates women or is racist, will be more carefully understood. Meaning-making in homes will be respected and understood as not just being about books, but will be recognized as being about family traditions, intergenerational literacies, and multilingual literacies. The 'stuff' of literacy will be respected and the ways in which literacies are embodied in print, textiles, digital stuff, including mobile phones, cameras and videogames, will become more important. Teachers can link these home literacies to the curriculum and links between online and offline spaces will be more securely established and recognized. Writing on the computer will not be separated off as 'ICT', but will be fully congruent with all literacy practices in community contexts.

Third, students will be encouraged to develop critical literacy skills that are in place (Morrell, 2008; Comber, 2010). This will involve taking images of neighbourhoods, counting, for example, the stores that sell alcohol over the stores that sell books. Spatial literacies will become more important. This understanding will also link to sustainability and an agenda that is about reducing carbon footprints. Schools will work with policy-makers to track the neighbourhood's characteristics. Literacy will involve the skills of GPS mapping and *Google Earth* as well as deciding what things count in communities for literacy learning. Schools will become hubs for research on literacy and rather than teach pre-set skills, the literacy curriculum will be the subject of research and inquiry. In that way, literacy will be seen as *cultural* (i.e., embedded in contexts), *critical* (i.e., as a source of power relations and also a site of critique), and also *operational* (i.e., as something to be learned) (Green, 1998).

Fourth, digital and immersive worlds will become more prevalent, more naturalized and more accepted as *the* forum for communication and understanding. What this increased ubiquity means is that our engagement with texts and with literacy will shift. Texts have changed dramatically over the past decade and where we previously turned pages, we now scroll, touch, tap, slide, etc. With these shifts in the formats, designs, and functions of texts and devices that hold texts, there needs to be similar, commensurate shifts in classroom practice. What is more, there needs to be a shift in the kinds of media and tools that we use in the classroom, such as more use of tablets and mobile devices. The kinds of literacy practices that we adopt in digital environments need to be far more present in literacy curriculum and teaching.

Fifth, and connected to the above point, educators need a language and a logic for new communicative practices that are multimodal and participatory. Notions such as remix, mash-ups, participating in online chat, collaborative work, problem-solving will (or should) become standard and accepted parlance for literacy work in primary, middle and secondary classrooms. Working with and across different modes should be part of everyday teaching so that students move far more fluidly from their modally complex lives outside school walls to their worlds within school walls. But what is to become of spelling, grammar, mechanics, as they are still alive and well in written composition? These more traditional skills still figure in the world of reading, writing and composition, and as literacy educators we need to find new ways of presenting conventions so that students can navigate the rapidity of change with enduring ways of communicating.

Finally, there is a need to shift our logic and language for literacy education. Design and thinking about design literacies is one way forward. Teaching reading, writing, speaking, listening through design is more in line with the sorts of skills and texts that students regularly inhabit. Having students work collaboratively on and offline fosters more permability between being in and out of school. A big challenge for educators broadly, and literacy educators specifically, is developing assessment frameworks that assess digital, multimodal, design-based skills. We have some way to go in developing curriculum, pedagogy and assessment measures shaped around twenty-first-century practices.

- What are the gaps you see in your practice between the curricula and the literacies your students use?

Final vignette: A winter's day made for innovation

To conclude the second edition, we offer a classroom moment from field-notes from March 2, 2011 in a secondary school in Toronto, Canada.

I (Jennifer) arrived at 1:30 and prepped for the lesson. The students looked so tired. After entering, some of the students put their heads on their desks. Others checked their mobile phones. Still others stared off vacantly. I think that it may be winter blues or just fatigue. Eryn and I had planned a fun lesson using arts and crafts to make a twenty-first-century invention. Eryn did most of the planning (and I was worried that it would be too primary for 16-year-olds). Eryn brought colourful chart paper, markers, stickers, glue, pipe cleaners, fuzz balls, etc. We created stations for students to work with the materials to create something. Surprisingly, at least for me, the students perked up and loved working with arts and crafts, making something with their hands on their own. They were tired of group activities, they were tired of pen-and-paper activities, they were even tired of media and watching *YouTube* videos. They loved the idea of using arts and crafts to produce visuals of technology and media-driven inventions. After Eryn gave directions and then I spoke about design principles and Eryn spoke with a couple of students who were late, all 13 students worked away on hallographic cellphones and 3-D videogames and rotating television screens. It was noisy, but most of the noise came from students finishing up and circulating to see what their peers had created. What I remarked during the lesson is that each student knew exactly what they were going to invent and were incredibly creative about it.

I sat with each student, with the exception of two students who were too engrossed to chat with me. We talked about functionality and design principles. In other words, we talked about how their invention works and what it will look like. Suddenly, it was 3:00 and we didn't finish what we needed to finish. For the next class, students were going to present their inventions to the group.

Yet again, I remarked on student creativity and their capacity to innovate.

References

Abrams, S.S. (2010). The dynamics of videogaming: Influences affecting game play and learning. In P. Zemliansky and D. Wilcox (Eds), *Theoretical and Practical Perspectives*, USA: IGI Global, pp. 78–90.

Alvermann, D. (Ed.) (2002). *Adolescents in digital worlds*. New York: Peter Lang.

Alvermann, D. E. (2008). Commentary: why bother theorizing adolescents' online literacies for classroom practice and research? *Journal of Adolescent & Adult Literacy, 52*, 8–19.

Anderson, J., Anderson, A., Friedrich, N., & Kim, J. (2010). Taking stock of family literacy: some contemporary perspectives. *Journal of Early Childhood Literacy, 10*(1), 33–53.

Anning, A. (2003). Pathways to the Graphicacy Club: the crossroad of home and pre-school. *Journal of Early Childhood Literacy, 3*(1), 5–35.

Bailey, M., Harrison, C., & Brooks, G. (2002). The Boots Books for Babies Project: impact on library registration and book loans. *Journal of Early Childhood Literacy, 2*(1), 45–64.

Ballenger, C. (1999). *Teaching other people's children: literacy and learning in a bilingual classroom*. New York: Teachers College Press.

Barton, D., & Hamilton, M. (1998). *Local literacies: reading and writing in one community*. London: Routledge.

Barton, D. (2001). Directions for literary research: analysing language and literacy practices in a textually mediated world. *Language and Education, 15*(2 and 3), 91–204.

Bearne, E. (2003). Rethinking literacy: communication, representation and text. *Reading: Literacy and Language, 37*(3), 98–103.

Bearne, E., & Bazalgette, C. (2010). *Beyond words: developing children's response to multimodal texts*. London: CLPE and UKLA.

Black, A. (2009). Online fanfiction, global identities, and imagination. *Research in the Teaching of English, 43*(4), 397–425.

Blackledge, A. (2000). Power relations and the social construction of 'literacy' and 'illiteracy': the experience of Bangladeshi women in Birmingham. In M. Martin-Jones and K. Jones (Eds.), *Multilingual literacies: reading and writing different worlds*. Amsterdam: John Benjamins Ltd., pp. 37–54.

Blackledge, A., & Creese, A. (2010). *Multilingualism*. London: Continuum.

Bourdieu, P. (1990). *The logic of practice*. Trans. R. Nice. Cambridge: Polity Press.

Brandt, D., & Clinton, K. (2002). The limits of the local: expanding perspectives of literacy as a social practice. *Journal of Literacy Research, 34*(3), 337–356.

Brandt, D., & Clinton, K. (2006). Afterword. In K. Pahl & J. Rowsell (Eds.), *Travel notes from the New Literacy Studies: instances of practice*. Clevedon, UK: Multilingual Matters Ltd., pp. 254–258.

Brooke, R. E. (Ed.). (2003). *Rural voices: place-conscious education and the teaching of writing*. New York: Teachers College Press.

Brooks, G., Gorman, T., Harman, D., & Wilkin, A. (1996). *Family literacy works*. London: BSA.

Browne, A. (2001). *Voices in the park*. London: DK Children.

Burnett, C., & Myers, J. (2002). 'Beyond the frame': exploring children's literacy practices. *Reading: Literacy and Language, 36*(2), 56–62.

Campano, G. (2007). *Immigrant students and literacy: reading, writing, and remembering*. New York: Teachers College Press.

Carrington, V. (2003). 'I'm in a bad mood. Let's go shopping': interactive dolls, consumer culture and a 'glocalized' model of literacy. *Journal of Early Childhood Literacy, 3*(1), 83–98.

Carrington, V. (2005). New textual landscapes, information and early literacy. In J. Marsh (Ed.), *Popular culture, new media and digital literacy in early childhood*. Abingdon: Routledge/Falmer, pp. 13–27.

Chandler-Olcott, K., & Mahar, D. (2003). Tech-savviness meets multiliteracies: exploring adolescent girls' technology-mediated literacy practices. *Reading Research Quarterly, 38*(3), 356–385.

Christensen, L. (2009). *Teaching for joy and justice: re-imagining the language arts classroom*. Milwaukee, WI: Rethinking Schools.

Christiansen, P., & O'Brien, M. (Eds.) (2003). *Children in the city: home, neighbourhood and community*. London: Routledge.

Clark, A. (2010). *Transforming children's spaces*. London: Routledge.

Clark, E., Kjorholt, A. T., & Moss, P. (Eds.) (2005). *Beyond listening: children's perspectives on early childhood services*. Bristol: The Policy Press.

Clay, M. (1975). *What did I write? Beginning writing behaviour*. London: Heinemann.

Cochran-Smith, M., & Lytle, S. L. (2009). *Inquiry as stance: practitioner research in the next generation*. New York: Teachers College Press.

Coiro, J., Knobel, M., Lankshear, C., & Leu, D. (Eds.) (2008). *The handbook of research in new literacies*. Mahwah, NJ: Lawrence Erlbaum Associates.

Collins, J. P., Slembrouck, S., & Baynham, M. (2009). *Globalization and language in contact*. London & New York: Continuum.

Comber, B. (2007). Assembling dynamic repertoires of literate practices: teaching that makes a difference. In J. Marsh & E. Bearne (Eds.), *Literacy and social inclusion: closing the gap*. London: Trentham Press, pp. 115–131.

Comber, B. (2010). Critical literacies in place: teachers who work for just and sustainable communities. In J. Lavia & M. Moore (Eds.), *Cross-cultural perspectives on policy and practice: decolonizing community contexts*. London: Routledge, pp. 43–57.

Comber, B., Nixon, H., & Reid, J. (Eds.) (2007). *Literacies in place: teaching environmental communications*. Newtown, NSW: Primary English Teaching Association.

Comber, B., Thomson, P., & Wells, M. (2001). Critical Literacy finds a 'place': writing and social action in a low-income Australian Grade 2–3 classroom. *The Elementary School Journal, 101*(4), 451–464.

Compton-Lilly, C. (2007). *Rereading families: the literate lives of urban children, the intermediate years*. New York: Teachers College Press.

Compton-Lilly, C. (2010). Considering time: in the field of family literacy and in the lives of families. In K. Dunsmore & D. Fisher (Eds.), *Bringing literacy home*. Newark, DE: International Reading Association, pp. 306–331.

Compton-Lilly, C., & Greene, S. (Eds.) (2011). *Bedtime stories and book reports: connecting parent involvement and family literacy*. New York: Teachers College Press.

Connerton, P. (1989). *How societies remember*. Cambridge: Cambridge University Press.

Cope, B., & Kalantzis, M. (Eds.) (2000). *Multiliteracies: literacy learning and the design of social futures*. London: Routledge.

Cope, B. & Kalantzis M. (2004). *Putting multiltieracies to the test*, www.alea.edu.au/documents/item/59 (accessed September 2, 2011).

Corbett, M. (2007). *Learning to leave: the irony of schooling in a coastal community.* Halifax, Nova Scotia: Fernwood Publishers.

Davies, J. (2006). Escaping the borderlands: an exploration of the internet as a cultural space for teenaged Wiccan girls. In K. Pahl & J. Rowsell (Eds.), *Travel notes from the New Literacy Studies.* Clevedon, UK: Multilingual Matters.

Davies, J., & Merchant, G. (2009). *Web2 for schools.* New York: Peter Lang.

Dunsmore, K., & Fisher, D. (Eds.) (2010). *Bringing literacy home.* Newark, DE: International Reading Association.

Dyson, A. H. (2003). *The brothers and sisters learn to write: popular literacies in childhood and school cultures.* New York: Teachers College Press.

Early Education and Care: English Curriculum Framework for New Brunswick. (2007). www.unbf.ca/education/ecc/childcareCurriculum/Framework.pdf (accessed September 4, 2011).

Evangelou, M., Sylva, K., & Myriacou, M., with Wild, M., & Glenny, G. (2009). *Early years learning and development: a literature review.* Research Report DCSF-RR176. London: Crown Copyright.

Facer, K. (2011). *Learning futures: education technology and social change.* London: Routledge.

Flewitt, R. (2008). Multimodal literacies. In J. Marsh & E. Hallet (Eds.), *Desirable literacies: approaches to language and literacy in the early years.* London: Sage, pp. 122–139.

Gay, G. (2000). *Culturally responsive teaching: theory, research and practice.* New York: Teachers College Press.

Gee, J. P. (1996). *Social literacies and linguistics.* London: Routledge.

Gee, J. P. (1999a). Reading and the new literacy studies: reframing the National Academy of Sciences report on reading. *Journal of Literacy Research, 31,* 355–374.

Gee, J. P. (1999b). *An introduction to discourse analysis: theory and method.* London: Routledge.

Gee, J. P. (2003). *What video games have to teach us about learning and literacy.* New York: Palgrave Macmillan.

Genishi, C., & Dyson, A. H. (2009). *Children, language, & literacy: diverse learners in diverse times.* New York: Teachers College Press.

Gonzalez, N., Moll, L., & Amanti C. (Eds.) (2005). *Funds of knowledge: theorizing practices in households, communities and classrooms.* Mahwah, NJ: Lawrence Erlbaum Associates.

Graham, L. (2009). It was a challenge but we did it! Digital worlds in a primary classroom. *Literacy, 43*(2), 107–114.

Green, B. (1998). The new literacy challenge. *Literacy Learning: Secondary Thoughts, 7*(1), 36–46.

Greenhough, P., Scanlan, M., Feiler, A., Johnson, D., Yee, W. C., Andrews, J., Price, A., Smithson, M., & Hughes, M. (2005). Boxing clever: using shoeboxes to support home–school knowledge exchange. *Literacy, 39*(2), 97–103.

Gregory, E. (2001). Sisters and brothers as language and literacy teachers: synergy between siblings. *Journal of Early Childhood Literacy, 1*(3), 301–322.

Gregory, E. (2008). *Learning to read in a new language: making sense of words and worlds.* New York: Sage.

Gregory, E., Arju, T., Jessel, J., Kenner, C., & Ruby, M. (2007). Snow White in disguise: interlingual and intercultural exchanges between grandparents and young children at home in East London. *Journal of Early Childhood Literacy, 7*(1), 5–25.

Gregory, E., Long, S., & Volk, D. (Eds.). (2004). *Many pathways to literacy: young children learning with siblings, grandparents, peers, communities.* London: Routledge.

Gregory, E., & Williams, A. (2000). Work or play? Unofficial literacies in the lives of two East London communities. In M. Martin-Jones & K. Jones (Eds.), *Multilingual literacies: reading and writing different worlds*. Amsterdam: John Benjamins, pp. 37–54.

Gutiérrez, K., & Stone, L. D. (2000). Synchronic and diachronic dimensions of social practice: an emerging methodology for cultural-historical perspectives on literacy learning. In C. Lee & P. Smagorinsky (Eds.), *Vygotskian perspectives on literacy research: constructing meaning through collaborative inquiry*. New York: Cambridge University Press, pp.150–165.

Gutiérrez, K. D. (2008). Developing a sociocritical literacy in the third space. *Reading Research Quarterly, 43*(2), 148–164.

Gutiérrez, K. D., Baquedano-Lopez, P., Tejeda, C., & Rivera, A. (1999). Building a culture of collaboration through hybrid language practices. *Theory into Practice, 38*, 87–93.

Gutiérrez, K. D., & Rogoff, B. (2003). Cultural ways of learning: individual traits for repertoires of practice. *Educational Researcher, 32*(5), 19–25.

Hannon, P., & Nutbrown, C. (1997). Teachers' use of a conceptual framework for early literacy education with parents. *Teacher Development, 1*(3), 405–420.

Heath, S. B. (1983). *Ways with words: language, life and work in communities and classrooms*. Cambridge: Cambridge University Press.

Hill, S. (2010). The millennium generation: teacher-researchers exploring new forms of literacy. *Journal of Early Childhood Literacy, 10*(3), 314–340.

Holland, D., Lachicotte, W., Skinner, D., & Cain, C. (2001, Second Printing). *Identity and agency in cultural worlds*. Cambridge, MA: Harvard University Press.

Holland, D., & Lave, J. (Eds.) (2001). *History in person: enduring struggles, contentious practice, intimate identities*. Sante Fe, NM: School of American Research Press.

Hull, G., & Shultz, K. (Eds.) (2002). *School's out! Bridging out-of-school literacies*. New York: Teachers College Press.

Hurdley, R. (2006). Dismantling mantelpieces: narrating identities and materializing culture in the home. *Sociology, 40*(4), 717–733.

Hymes, D. (Ed.) (1996). *Ethnography, linguistics, narrative inequality: towards an understanding of voice*. London: Routledge.

Ingold, T. (2007). *Lines: a brief history*. London: Routledge.

Janks, H. (2010). *Literacy and power*. London: Routledge.

Jewitt, C. (Ed.) (2009). *The Routledge handbook of multimodal analysis*. London: Routledge.

Jewitt, C., & Kress, G. (Eds.) (2003). *Multimodal literacy*. New York: Peter Lang.

Kenner, C. (2000). *Home pages: literacy links for bilingual children*. Stoke on Trent: Trentham Books.

Kenner, C. (2004). *Becoming biliterate*. Stoke on Trent: Trentham Books.

Kim, J., & Anderson, J. (2008). Mother–child shared reading in print and digital texts. *Journal of Early Childhood Literacy, 8*, 213–245.

Kind, S. (2010). Art encounters: movements in the visual arts and early childhood education. In V. Pacini-Ketchabaw (Ed.), *Flows, rhythms, & intensities of early childhood education curriculum*. New York: Peter Lang, pp. 113–131.

Kinloch, V. (2010). *Harlem on our minds: place, race and the literacies of urban youth*. New York: Teachers College Press.

Knobel, M., & Lankshear, C. (2007). *A new literacies sampler*. New York: Peter Lang.

Kress, G. (1997). *Before writing: rethinking the paths to literacy*. London: Routledge.

Kress, G. (2010). *Literacy in the new media age*. London: Routledge.

Kress, G., & Van Leeuwen, T. (1996). *Reading images: the grammar of visual design*. London: Routledge.

Lancaster, L. (2003). Beginning at the beginning: how a young child constructs time multimodally. In C. Jewitt & G. Kress (Eds.), *Multimodal literacy*. New York: Peter Lang, pp. 107–122.

Lanham, R. (1995). *The electronic word: democracy, technology and the arts.* New York: Peter Lang.

Lankshear, C., & Knobel, M. (2006). *New literacies: everyday practices and classroom learning* (second edition). Maidenhead: McGraw Hill/Open University Press.

Larson, J., & Marsh, J. (2005). *Making literacy real: theories and practices for learning and teaching.* London: Sage.

Latour, B. (1996). *Aramis, or the love of technology.* Cambridge: Harvard University Press.

Lave, J., & Wenger, E. (1991). *Situated learning.* Cambridge: Cambridge University Press.

Leander, K. M. (2002). Locating Latanya: the situated production of identity artifacts in classroom interaction. *Research in the Teaching of English, 37,* 198–250.

Leander, K. M., & Sheehy, M. (Eds.) (2004). *Spatializing literacy research and practice.* New York: Peter Lang.

Lee, C. D. (2008). The centrality of culture to the scientific study of learning and development: how an ecological framework in education research facilitates civic responsibility. *Educational Researcher, 37,* 267.

Levy, R. (2011). *Young children reading at home and at school.* London: Sage.

Luke, A., & Carrington, V. (2002). Globalisation, literacy, curriculum practice. In R. Fisher, G. Brooks & M. Lewis (Eds.), *Raising standards in Literacy.* London: Routledge/Falmer, pp. 231–250.

Luke, A. (2005). Foreword. In K. Pahl & J. Rowsell (Eds.), *Literacy and education: Understanding the New Literacy Studies in the classroom.* London: Sage.

Mackey, M. (2010). Reading from the feet up: the local work of literacy. *Children's Literature in Education, 41,* 323–339.

Marsh, J. (2003). Early childhood literacy and popular culture. In N. Hall et al. (Eds.), *Handbook of early childhood literacy.* London: Sage.

Marsh, J. (Ed.) (2005). Children of the digital age. In J. Marsh (Ed.), *Popular culture, new media and digital literacy in early childhood.* Abingdon: Routledge/Falmer, pp. 1–10.

Marsh, J. (2006). Popular culture in the literacy curriculum: A Bourdieusian analysis. *Reading Research Quarterly, 41*(2), 160–174.

Marsh, J. (2011). Young children's literacy practices in a virtual world: establishing an online interaction order. *Reading Research Quarterly, 42*(6), 101–111.

Marsh, J., & Thompson, P. (2001). Parental involvement in literacy development: using media texts. *Journal of Research in Reading, 24*(3), 266–278.

Massey, D. (2005). *For space.* London: Routledge.

McNaughton, S. (2001). Constructing expertise: the development of parents' and teachers' ideas about literacy practices and the transition to school. *Journal of Early Childhood Literacy, 1*(1), 40–58.

Merchant, G. (2007). Digital writing in the early years. In J. Coiro, M. Knobel, C. Lankshear & D. Leu (Eds.), *The handbook of research on new literacies.* Mahwah, NJ: Lawrence Erlbaum Associates.

Michaels, S. (1986). Narrative presentations: an oral preparation for literacy with 1st Graders. In J. Cook-Gumperz (Ed.), *The social construction of literacy.* Cambridge: Cambridge University Press, pp. 94–116.

Millard, E. (2003). Towards a literacy of fusion: new times, new teaching and learning? *Reading: Literacy and Language, 37*(1), 3–9.

Miller, D. (2008). *The comfort of things.* Cambridge: Polity Press.

Miller, D. (2010). *Stuff.* London: Routledge.

Moje, E. B. (2000). Circles of kinship, friendship, position, and power: examining the community in community-based literacy research. *Journal of Literacy Research, 32*(1), 77–112.

Moje, E. B., Ciechanowski, K. M., Kramer, K., Ellis, L., Carrillo, R., & Collazo, T. (2004). Working toward third space in content area literacy: an exploration of everyday funds of knowledge and Discourse. *Reading Research Quarterly, 39*(1), 38–70.

Moll, L., Amanti, C., Neff, D., & Gonzalez, N. (1992). Funds of knowledge for teaching: using a qualitative approach to connect homes and classrooms. *Theory into Practice, 31*(2), 132–141.

Morrell, E. (2008). *Critical literacy and urban youth: pedagogies of access, dissent and liberation.* London and New York: Routledge.

Muspratt, S., Luke, A., & Freebody, P. (1997). *Constructing critical literacies.* Sydney: Allen & Unwin.

Neuman, S. B., & Celano, D. (2001). Access to print in low-income and middle-income communities: an ecological study of four neighbourhoods. *Reading Research Quarterly, 36*(1), 8–26.

Neuman, S. B., & Celano, D. (2006). The knowledge gap: implications of levelling the playing field for low-income and middle-income children. *Reading Research Quarterly, 41*(2), 176–201.

Nichols, S. (2011). Young children's literacy in the activity space of the library: a geosemiotic investigation. *Journal of Early Childhood Literacy, 30*(2), 164–189.

Nichols, S., Nixon, H., & Rowsell, J. (2009). Shaping the identities and practices in relation to early years literacy. *Literacy, 43*(2), 65–74.

Nixon, H. (2007). Expanding the semiotic repertoire: environmental communications in the primary school. *Australian Journal of Language and Literacy, 30*(2), 102–117.

Nixon, H. (2011). From bricks to clicks: hybrid commercial spaces in the landscape of early childhood literacy learning. *Journal of Early Childhood Literacy, 11*, 114–140.

Nixon, H., & Comber, B. (2006). The differential recognition of children's cultural practices in middle primary literacy classrooms. *Literacy, 40*(3), 127–136.

Nixon, J., Allan, J., & Mannion, G. (2001). Educational renewal as democratic practice: 'new' community schooling in Scotland. *International Journal of Inclusive Education, 5*(4), 329–352.

Norton, B. (2010). Language and identity. In N. Hornberger & S. McKay (Eds.), *Sociolinguistics and language education.* Bristol, UK: Multilingual Matters, pp. 349–369.

Nutbrown, C., Hannon, P., & Morgan, A. (2005). *Early literacy work with families: policy, practice and research.* London: Sage.

Orellana, M. (1999). Space and place in an urban landscape: learning from children's views of their social worlds. *Visual Sociology, 14*, 73–89.

Pahl, K. (1999). *Transformations: making meaning in nursery education.* Stoke on Trent and London: Trentham Books.

Pahl, K. (2002). Ephemera, mess and miscellaneous piles: texts and practices in families. *Journal of Early Childhood Literacy, 2*(2), 145–165.

Pahl, K. (2004). Narratives, artifacts and cultural identities: an ethnographic study of communicative practices in homes. *Linguistics and Education, 15*(4), 339–358.

Pahl, K. (2005). Narrative spaces and multiple identities: children's textual explorations of console games in home settings. In J. Marsh (Ed.), *Popular culture, media and digital literacies in early childhood.* London: Routledge/Falmer, pp. 126–145.

Pahl, K. (2007). Creativity in events and practices: a lens for understanding children's multimodal texts. *Literacy, 41*(2), 86–92.

Pahl, K., & Allan C. (2011). I don't know what literacy is: uncovering hidden literacies in a community library using ecological and participatory methodologies with children. *Journal of Early Childhood Literacy, 11*(2), 190–213.

Pahl, K., with Kelly, S. (2005). Family literacy as a third space between home and school. *Literacy, 39*(2), 91–96.

Pahl, K., Lewis, M., & Ritchie, L. (2010). Book sharing in the home: an ethnographic study. Unpublished report for Booktrust, June.

Pahl, K., Lewis, M., & Ritchie, L. (2011). The Inspire Rotherham final report. Unpublished report for Inspire Rotherham.

Pahl, K., & Pollard, A. (2010). The case of the disappearing object: narratives and artefacts in homes and a museum exhibition from Pakistani heritage families in South Yorkshire. *Museum and Society, 8*(1), 1–17.

Pahl, K., & Rowsell, J. (2005). *Literacy and education: the new literacy studies in the classroom.* London: Paul Chapman.

Pahl, K., & Rowsell, J. (2010). *Artifactual literacies: every object tells a story.* New York: Teachers College Press.

Pink, S. (2009). *Doing sensory ethnography.* London: Sage.

Potter, J. (2010). Embodied memory and curatorship in children's digital media production. *English Teaching: Practice and Critique, 9*(May), 22–35.

Pratt, M. L. (1992). *Imperial eyes: travel writing and transculturation.* London and New York: Routledge.

QCA. (2004). *More than words: multimodal texts in the classroom.* London: UKLA/QCA.

Rodriguez-Brown, F.V. (2010). Latino culture and schooling: reflections on family literacy with a culturally and linguistically different community. In K. Dunsmore & D. Fisher (Eds.), *Bringing literacy home.* Newark, DE: International Reading Association, pp. 203–225.

Rogers, R. (2003). *A critical discourse analysis of family literacy practices: power in and out of print.* Mahwah, NJ: Lawrence Erlbaum Associates.

Rogers, R., Mosley, M., Kramer, M. A., & The Literacy for Social Justice Teacher Research Group. (2009). *Designing socially just learning communities.* London: Routledge.

Rosowsky, A. (2001). Decoding as a cultural practice and its effects on the reading process of bilingual pupils. *Language and Education, 15*(1), 56–70.

Rosowsky, A. (2008). *Heavenly readings: liturgical literacy in a multilingual context.* Bristol: Multilingual Matters.

Rowsell, J. (2000). British and Canadian perspectives on educational publishing: Texts as Traces of Social Practice. Unpublished Ph.D. London: King's College Press.

Rowsell, J. (forthcoming). *Doing multimodality: The New Literacies.* London: Routledge.

Rowsell, J., & Pahl, K. (2007). Sedimented identities in texts: instances of practice. *Reading Research Quarterly, 42*(3), 388–401.

Samuel, R., & Thompson, P. (Eds.) (1990). *The myths we live by.* London: Routledge.

Saxena, M. (2000). Taking account of history and culture in community-based research on multilingual literacy. In M. Martin-Jones & K. Jones (Eds.), *Multilingual literacies: reading and writing different worlds.* Amsterdam: John Benjamins, pp. 275–298.

Scanlan, M. (2008). My story in a box: linking home and school to explore identity, creativity, writing and oracy. Unpublished doctoral dissertation, University of Bristol, UK.

Scanlan, M. (2010). Opening the box: Literacy, artefacts and identity. *Literacy, 44*(1), 28–36.

Schamroth-Abrams, S., & Rowsell, J. (2011). *Rethinking identity and literacy education in the 21st century. National Society for the Study of Education Yearbook. 110*(1). New York: Teachers College Press.

Schultz, K. (2002). Looking across space and time: reconceptualizing literacy learning in and out of School. *Research in the Teaching of English, 36*, 356–390.

Scribner, S., & Cole, M. (1981). *The psychology of literacy.* Cambridge, MA: Harvard University Press.

Sheridan, M.P., & Rowsell, J. (2010). *Design literacies: learning and innovation in a digital age.* London: Routledge.

Siegal, M. (2006). Rereading the signs of multimodality. *Language Arts, 84*(1), 65.

Simon, R. (2005). Bridging life and learning through inquiry and improvisation: literacy practices at a model high school. In B. V. Street (Ed.), *Literacies across educational contexts.* Philadelphia, PA: Caslon, pp. 124–144.

Simon, R. (2009). Constructing a language of learning to teach. In M. Cochran-Smith & S. L. Lytle (Eds.), *Inquiry as stance: practitioner research in the next generation.* New York: Teachers College Press, pp. 275–292.

Simon, R. (2012). 'Without comic books there would be no me': Teachers as connoisseurs of adolescents' literate lives. *Journal of Adolescent and Adult Literacy, 55*(6), 516–526.

Snow, C., Burns, S., & Griffin, P. (1998). *Preventing reading difficulties in young children.* Washington, DC: The National Academies Press.

Soja, E. (2010). *Seeking spatial justice.* Minneapolis, MN: University of Minnesota Press.

Stein, P. (2007). *Multimodal pedagogies in diverse classrooms: representation, rights and resources.* London: Routledge.

Steinkuehler, C., & King, E. (2009). Digital literacies for the disengaged: creating after school contexts to support boys' game-based literacy skills. *On the Horizon, 17*(1), 47–59.

Street, B. V. (Ed.) (1993a). Culture is a verb: anthropological aspects of language and cultural process. In D. L. Gradoll et al. (Eds.), *Language and culture.* Clevedon, UK: BAAL and Multilingual Matters, pp. 24–44.

Street, B. V. (Ed.) (1993b). *Cross-cultural approaches to literacy.* Cambridge: Cambridge University Press.

Street, B. V. (Ed.) (1995). *Social literacies: critical approaches to literacy in development, ethnography, and education.* Harlow: Pearson Education.

Street, B. V. (Ed.) (2005). *Literacies across educational contexts: mediating learning and teaching.* Philadelphia, PA: Caslon.

Street, B.V., & Street, J. (1991). The schooling of literacy. In D. Barton & R. Ivanic (Eds.), *Writing in the community.* London: Sage, pp. 143–166.

Taylor, D. (1983). *Family literacy: young children learning to read and write.* Portsmouth, NH: Heinemann.

Thomas, D., & Seely Brown, J. (2011). *A new culture of learning: cultivating the imagination for a world of constant change.* Palo Alto, CA: Stanford University Press.

Tizard, B., & Hughes, M. (1984). *Young children learning: talking and thinking at home and at school.* London: Fontana.

Uprichard, E. (2008). Children as 'being and becoming': children, childhood and temporality. *Children and Society, 22*, 303–313.

Vasudevan, L. (2006). Looking for angels: knowing adolescents by engaging with their multimodal literacy practices. *Journal of Adolescent & Adult Literacy, 50*(4), 252–256.

Vasudevan, L. (2009). Performing new geographies of literacy teaching and learning. *English Education, 41*(4), 356–374.

Volk, D. (1997). Continuities and discontinuities: teaching and learning in the home and school of a Puerto Rican five year old. In E. Gregory (Ed.), *One child, many worlds: early learning in multicultural communities.* London: David Fulton Publishers, pp. 47–62.

Vygotsky, L. (1978). *Mind in society: the development of higher psychological processes.* Cambridge, MA: Harvard University Press.

Walsh, M. (2003). Reading pictures: what do they reveal? Young children's reading of visual texts. *Literacy, 37*(3), 123–130.

Walsh, M. (2011). *Multimodal literacy: researching classroom practice.* Sydney: e:lit, Primary Teachers Association of Australia.

Walsh, M., & Simpson, A. (2010). Research into the teaching of reading and learning. *English Education, 4*(14), 356–374.

Wells, G. (1986). *The meaning makers: children learning language and using language to learn.* Portsmouth, NH: Heinemann.

Wells, G., & Claxton, G. (Eds.) (2002). *Learning for life in the 21st century.* Malden, MA: Blackwell.

Whitty, P., Rose, S., Baisley, D., Comeau, L., & Thompson, A. (2008). Honouring educators' co-construction of picture books. *Child Study, 33*(2), 21–23.

Wilson, A. (2000). There is no escape from third space theory: borderline discourse and the 'in between' literacies of prisons. In D. Barton, M. Hamilton & R. Ivanic (Eds.), *Situated literacies: reading and writing in context.* London: Routledge, pp. 54–69.

Wohlwend, K. (2009). Damsels in discourse: girls consuming and producing identity texts through Disney princess play. *Reading Research Quarterly, 44*(1), 57–83.

Wohlwend, K. (2010). A is for avatar: young children in literacy 2.0 worlds and literacy 1.0 schools. *Language Arts, 88*(2), 144–152.

Yamada-Rice, D. (2010). Beyond words: an enquiry into children's home visual communication practices. *Journal of Early Childhood Literacy, 10*(3), 241–363.

Index

Note: Page references in **bold** type relate to glossary entries

Printed in Poland
by Amazon Fulfillment
Poland Sp. z o.o., Wrocław